Living in Nazi Germany

Elaine Halleck, *Book Editor*

Daniel Leone, *President*
Bonnie Szumski, *Publisher*
Scott Barbour, *Managing Editor*

GREENHAVEN PRESS®

San Diego • Detroit • New York • San Francisco • Cleveland
New Haven, Conn. • Waterville, Maine • London • Munich

© 2004 by Greenhaven Press. Greenhaven Press is an imprint of The Gale Group, Inc., a division of Thomson Learning, Inc.

Greenhaven® and Thomson Learning™ are trademarks used herein under license.

For more information, contact
Greenhaven Press
27500 Drake Rd.
Farmington Hills, MI 48331-3535
Or you can visit our Internet site at http://www.gale.com

ALL RIGHTS RESERVED.
No part of this work covered by the copyright hereon may be reproduced or used in any form or by any means—graphic, electronic, or mechanical, including photocopying, recording, taping, Web distribution or information storage retrieval systems—without the written permission of the publisher.

Every effort has been made to trace the owners of copyrighted material.

Cover credit: © Austrian Archives/CORBIS
Library of Congress, 115
National Archives, 36, 60, 89, 137

LIBRARY OF CONGRESS CATALOGING-IN-PUBLICATION DATA

Living in Nazi Germany / Elaine Halleck, book editor.
   p. cm. — (Exploring cultural history)
   Includes bibliographical references and index.
   ISBN 0-7377-1731-9 (lib. : alk. paper) — ISBN 0-7377-1732-7 (pbk. : alk. paper)
    1. Germany—Social conditions—1933–1945. 2. Germany—Politics and government—1933–1945. I. Halleck, Elaine. II. Series.
DD256.6.L58 2004
943.086—dc22
                                               2003057961

Printed in the United States of America

Contents

Foreword	6
Introduction	8

Chapter 1: Life as a Target of Nazi Brutality

Chapter Preface — 20

1. Police Justice
   by Robert Gellately — 22
   In the early years of Nazi rule, petty criminals were sent to concentration camps without trials, capital punishment was expanded, "law and order" was touted, and dissent was harshly punished.

2. Living in a Concentration Camp
   by Eugene Kogon — 32
   Life was horrific for political prisoners, criminals, "asocials," and "inferior" groups locked up in Nazi Germany's many concentration camps.

3. Growing Up Black in Nazi Germany
   by Hans Massaquoi — 40
   A black German describes the experience of being rejected by the Hitler Youth, which he had hoped to join, thereby coming to understand the dehumanizing policies of the Nazis toward anyone who was different.

4. The Impact of the Nuremberg Laws
   by Cynthia Crane — 48
   Hitler's Nuremberg Laws, which curtailed the rights of Jews, had a far-ranging impact. Children of "mixed" marriages were defined as Jewish, even if the Jewish parent had converted to another religion.

Chapter 2: From the Perspective of the Powerful

Chapter Preface — 55

1. The Fuehrer's Everyday Life
   by Albert Speer   57
   Hitler's chief architect describes the Fuehrer's behavior during trips to the mountains and dinners with associates, including his mistress Eva Braun.

2. The Kommandant and His Wife
   by Gitta Sereny   63
   Through interviews and letters, the author sheds light on the thought processes of the commander of two Nazi extermination camps, and his wife.

3. Children of the Reich
   by Gitta Sereny   72
   The offspring of high-ranking Nazi officials suffered their own peculiar form of trauma, including extreme guilt and shame that followed them into adulthood.

4. The Hitler Youth
   by Alfons Heck   85
   A former leader in the Hitler Youth examines his introduction to politics as a child in 1932 and his enthusiastic participation in the stirring Nuremberg Party Congress of 1938.

Chapter 3: Propaganda and Cultural Control

Chapter Preface   100

1. The Propaganda Apparatus
   by Joseph Goebbels   103
   Nazi propaganda chief Joseph Goebbels kept a diary describing his efforts at policing intellectuals and the press inside Germany and trying to control opinion outside his country.

2. The Triumph of National Socialism
   by Adolf Hitler   113
   In a 1939 speech, Hitler trumpeted the accomplishments of Nazism: economic growth, a decline in unemployment, industrial regeneration, and a spirit of national unity.

3. Two Jewish Musicians Under the Nazi Regime
   by Martin Goldsmith   119
   As fear and violence escalated, a pair of Jewish-German
   musicians were artistically restricted and allowed to
   play only in an all-Jewish orchestra created by the
   Nazis.

4. The Survival of Jazz Under Nazism
   by Michael Kater   130
   Jazz was becoming the hot music in Germany when
   the Nazis came to power and suppressed this African
   American sound.

5. Mobilizing Germans for Economic Victory
   by Nicholas Levis   135
   To create jobs, the Nazis pushed construction of an
   express-highway system and cars such as the Volkswagen. These industrial programs became fronts for
   military production and financial swindles.

Chronology   142
For Further Research   150
Index   154

Foreword

Too often, history books and teachers place an overemphasis on events and dates. Students learn that key births, battles, revolutions, coronations, and assassinations occurred in certain years. But when many centuries separate these happenings from the modern world, they can seem distant, disconnected, even irrelevant.

The reality is that today's society is *not* disconnected from the societies that preceded it. In fact, modern culture is a sort of melting pot of various aspects of life in past cultures. Over the course of centuries and millennia, one culture passed on some of its traditions, in the form of customs, habits, ideas, and beliefs, to another, which modified and built on them to fit its own needs. That culture then passed on its own version of the traditions to later cultures, including today's. Pieces of everyday life in past cultures survive in our own lives, therefore. And it is often these morsels of tradition, these survivals of tried and true past experience, that people most cherish, take comfort in, and look to for guidance. As the great English scholar and archaeologist Sir Leonard Woolley put it, "We cannot divorce ourselves from our past. We are always conscious of precedents . . . and we let experience shape our views and actions."

Thus, for example, Americans and the inhabitants of a number of other modern nations can pride themselves on living by the rule of law, educating their children in formal schools, expressing themselves in literature and art, and following the moral precepts of various religions and philosophies. Yet modern society did not invent the laws, schools, literature, art, religions, and philosophies that pervade it; rather, it inherited these things from previous cultures. "Time, the great destroyer, is also the great preserver," the late, noted thinker Herbert J. Muller once observed. "It has preserved . . . the immense accumulation of products, skills, styles, customs, institutions, and ideas that make the man on the American street indebted to all the peoples of history, including some who never saw a street." In this way, ancient Mesopotamia gave the world its first cities and literature; ancient Egypt, large-scale architecture; ancient Israel, the formative concepts of Judaism,

Christianity, and Islam; ancient Greece, democracy, the theater, Olympic sports, and magnificent ceramics; ancient China, gunpowder and exotic fabrics; ancient Rome and medieval England, their pioneering legal systems; Renaissance Italy, great painting and sculpture; Elizabethan England, the birth of modern drama; and colonial America, the formative environments of the founders of the United States, the most powerful and prosperous nation in world history. Only by looking back on those peoples and how they lived can modern society understand its roots.

Not all the products of cultural history have been so constructive, however. Most ancient Greeks severely restricted the civil rights and daily lives of women, for instance; the Romans kept and abused large numbers of slaves, as did many Americans in the years preceding the Civil War; and Nazi Germany and the Soviet Union curbed or suppressed freedom of speech, assembly, and religion. Examining these negative aspects of life in various past cultures helps to expose the origins of many of the social problems that exist today; it also reminds us of the ever-present potential for people to make mistakes and pursue misguided or destructive social and economic policies.

The books in the Greenhaven Press Exploring Cultural History series provide readers with the major highlights of life in human cultures from ancient times to the present. The family, home life, food and drink, women's duties and rights, childhood and education, arts and leisure, literacy and literature, roads and means of communications, slavery, religious beliefs, and more are examined in essays grouped by theme. The essays in each volume have been chosen for their readability and edited to manageable lengths. Many are primary sources. These original voices from a past culture echo through the corridors of time and give the volume a strong feeling of immediacy and authenticity. The other essays are by historians and other modern scholars who specialize in the culture in question. An annotated table of contents, chronology, and extensive bibliography broken down by theme add clarity and context. Thus, each volume in the Greenhaven Press Exploring Cultural History series opens a unique window through which readers can gaze into a distant time and place and eavesdrop on life in a long vanished culture.

Introduction

Nazi Germany, a regime that lasted for only twelve years during the first half of the twentieth century (from 1933 to 1945), continues to arouse intense interest in the twenty-first century. Scholars have remarked that public fascination with the Nazi era has overshadowed all other aspects of German history and culture. In 2000 the sociologists Harold R. Kerbo and Hermann Strasser noted,

> In most American bookstores, shelves devoted to Germany are dominated by books on World War II, Nazism, Hitler, and the Holocaust. The bookshelves for France, China, Mexico, or any other major country have books on politics, economic issues, religions, and the entire range of subjects that could be expected about a society and nation. It is as if everything else about Germany doesn't matter or never happened. No other country is dominated by one subject or such a short period of its history.... Young Germans visiting or living in the United States know that no matter whom they meet, the dreaded subject will inevitably come up.[1]

There are many reasons for the persistence of this intense curiosity about the Nazi era. The fact that one man—Adolf Hitler—was able to accrue so much power and wield it to such destructive ends is compelling. Undeniably, the horrors of the era evoke a morbid curiosity in many people. But the most essential reason to document the era is to understand how the atrocities occurred and to help ensure that they never happen again.

One of the most striking aspects of Nazi Germany is the fact that such barbarism and horror occurred in an essentially modern nation. The incongruities of the era are striking. When we see photos of Germans of the era dressed in suits and ties or knee-length dresses and high heels or Germans driving in automobiles, we are perplexed. It is difficult to reconcile such images with other photos that show starved concentration camp victims, heaps of eyeglasses that the Nazis removed from their imprisoned victims in the process of murdering them in gas chambers, or images of vats containing dismembered human parts that doctors of the era used for gruesome experiments. The fact that the atrocities of the Nazi era occurred in a developed Western society—

similar to other advanced European nations as well as the United States—is certainly one of the reasons that Nazi Germany retains such a strong hold on the popular imagination.

"A New Man"

Many trends have given rise to the perception of Germany of the 1930s and 1940s as an advanced society. Nazi leaders depicted themselves as the creators of a progressive nation poised on the edge of a momentous social shift toward modernity. They viewed their era as bright with the prospect of hopeful changes that would usher in a wonderful new world free of the oppressing problems of the past. This world, according to some of their statements, was to be populated by nothing other than a new breed of humans—a superman, or *Übermensch*. According to historian Klaus P. Fischer, "The aim of this totalitarian state, Hitler [said] . . . was to produce a new godlike human being. This is why National Socialism [Nazism], according to Hitler, was more than just a political movement, even 'more than a religion: it is the will to create a new man.'"[2]

The establishment of a totalitarian state in order to create a superior race of people was not a progressive agenda, especially since it involved the systematic elimination of people deemed "undesirable." Nevertheless, the Nazis portrayed their mission as a plan to modernize Germany.

Despite the Nazis' distorted ideology, Germany did excel in modern sciences. For example, Germany was a leading nation in developing practical medical advancements that had immense value in the lives of ordinary people throughout the world. The German chemist and pathologist Gerhard Domagk discovered the first antibiotic, sulfanilamide. This important discovery greatly reduced infections, which were a leading cause of death. (Ironically, Domagk was unable to accept a Nobel Prize for his work because of a Nazi decree.)

Germany was also at the forefront of other modern developments, such as communication. The German Heinrich Hertz was a key figure in the invention of the radio. Even before the Nazi regime came to power, the nation brought radio broadcasting under state control. Later, the Nazi government encouraged manufacturing of cheap radio sets that could easily be purchased for the home. German-born Emile Berliner invented and patented the gramophone, or record player. By the time of the Nazi era, ordinary Germans purchased recordings of many types of music, including folk, classical, traditional German marching music and anthems, big band, swing, and jazz. Germans of the Nazi era also listened to music and news on the radio. Likewise, newspaper publishing was a going concern in Nazi Germany, and Germans were avid readers of the many newspapers available throughout the country.

A Modern Economy

Germany had also developed a modern economy by the Nazi era, as illustrated by the large-scale economic control measures taken by the German government to pull the nation out of a dismal economic tailspin during the 1930s. Nazi leaders were chafing under a severe depression that was made unbearable by the penalties that had been imposed against Germany by victor nations after World War I. The Nazi government early on made road building and auto manufacturing top priorities. These measures jump-started the German economy and were applauded by ordinary Germans because they dramatically reduced unemployment. Some of the results—the German expressway, or autobahn system, and the Volkswagen automobile—are still well known today. Some car manufacturing efforts of the Nazi era were the result of joint ventures with the U.S. auto firms General Motors and Ford, which further underscores the similarity between the economy of Germany and other modern nations.

The social and professional structure of the Nazi era also seems familiar to twenty-first-century observers. Germany had a middle class and, although it patterned itself after the old, feudal ruling class more than the middle classes of some other nations, it was nevertheless fairly large and strong. The professionals—including doctors and artisans—formed associations that were typical of modern professional groups. One of them was the Deutsche Werkbund (German Association of Craftsmen), which was formed early in the twentieth century and embraced advanced machine production processes.

Werkbund designers of products for everyday living—for example, home appliances —were particularly progressive. One of the logical consequences of the Werkbund was a famous German school for designers, the Bauhaus. This school, arguably the most well-known design school of the twentieth century, was a center of avant-garde design in typography, architecture, furniture, and other everyday products. Designers schooled at the Bauhaus aimed to reflect modern materials and machine processes and to be free of old-fashioned style constraints.

The existence of the Bauhaus was cut short in 1933 when Nazi city council members tried to remove Communist sympathizers, whom they called "Cultural Bolsheviks," from the Bauhaus and replace them with Nazis. At this, the Bauhaus faculty dissolved the school. Many leading Bauhaus architects and designers joined the flood of intellectuals who fled Nazi Germany for the United States and other countries.

Modernism and Totalitarianism

The fate of the Bauhaus contradicts the claim that the Nazis were promoters of modernism. True, one of the Nazis' notable successes was in streamlining Germany's economy, and Germany was noted as the birthplace of many modern innovations. But Hitler's famous taste for kitsch or unsophisticated styles, his embrace of grandiose but outdated architectural styles, and the Nazis' persecution of modern artists all demonstrate that Nazism at heart was not consistent with either modernism or traditionalism.

Rather than seeking to modernize Germany, the Nazis sought totalitarian control. Despite its modern characteristics, German society devolved into a reign of terror during the 1930s and early 1940s. In fact, many of the scientific, technological, and cultural advances that marked Germany as a modern nation were ultimately used not to promote progress, but to support the totalitarian Nazi regime, wage an unjust war, and conduct massive genocide.

For example, modern medical science, which was highly developed in Germany, was bent by the Nazis toward achieving totalitarian power. Along with leaders in other countries, Germans of the Nazi era glimpsed the possibility of achieving power over the forces of nature that created disease. Scientists working in the field of eugenics combined an interest in genetics with methods that aimed to improve the inherited characteristics of humans. A primary means for achieving genetic improvement was by discouraging propagation among the "unfit" and thereby preventing, for example, mental retardation, alcoholism, poverty, and promiscuity. German doctors were required by Nazi laws (although there was little opposition from the doctors) to ignore the tenet in the Hippocratic oath that protects doctor-patient confidentiality and to report their patients who had genetic diseases to authorities. The result was involuntary sterilization. Although Germany was not the only country where sterilization was practiced (eugenics policies in California resulted in the involuntary sterilization of more than twenty thousand people from 1909 through the 1960s), it was the worst offender. In addition, the Nazis instituted a euthanasia program in which they killed disabled peopled who were deemed "unfit life." The medical personnel who carried out these killings did so under the banner of the Aktion program, which became a training ground for the Nazi officials who went on to staff death camps. It is estimated that from sixty to eighty thousand Germans were killed, usually by injection, in the Aktion program.

Hardened by these practices, medical scientists in the Nazi-run camps went on to carry out morbid medical experiments. For example, prisoners (often from "undesirable" racial groups that the Nazis claimed were defiling the genetic pool) were subjected to slow death by freezing in order to gauge their physical reactions.

High Tech in the Service of Totalitarianism

Likewise, modern technological devices such as the radio were put to the task of achieving authoritarian power for the Nazis. Nazi leaders were fully aware that in order to carry out their aim of controlling the population, a steady stream of propaganda was necessary. Radio broadcasts, along with the censored newspapers that Germans read daily, were some of their primary propaganda outlets. The state-controlled radio stations of Nazi Germany fed the people a steady diet of music, entertainment, and news that was designed to create enthusiasm for and compliance with government policies. Many of Hitler's long, emotional speeches were broadcast and received by Germans on home radios that the government had helped to produce. According to Klaus P. Fischer,

Germans were inundated by a veritable blitzkrieg of verbal and musical clutter. Daily programming generally fell into three categories: political broadcasts, music, and radio plays. . . . All work stopped as people gathered in factories, taverns, party offices, and public squares to listen to government broadcasts. . . . Another innovation was special announcements, heralded by horn music from a one-hundred-man orchestra, followed by unctuous delivery of the great message, usually of another Nazi triumph, and polished off by a thanksgiving hymn, the national anthem, three minutes of silence, and more marching music.[3]

The Nazis viewed education as just another form of political propaganda. Most children and teenagers were compelled to join youth groups such as the Jungvolk (Young Germans), Jungmädel (Young Girls), and Hitler Youth. These organizations indoctrinated young people in Nazi ideology and included uniforms, outdoor activities, and some military training for boys. "Karl," who later became a U.S. citizen, recalls his experience in the Jungvolk:

> If there's a group of Boy Scouts in your neighborhood, you want to become a member, too. We were looking forward to going to meetings, because we had a sense of belonging that everybody wants to have. . . .
>
> Exercises, lectures in history, political lectures, the purity of the Aryan race [pure German race postulated by Nazis]—a lot of what in later life you think is garbage. There were a lot of good things in it. And a lot of nonsense that the political people were trying to brainwash you with.[4]

Modern economic and industrial practices that enabled the concentration of power in the hands of corporations throughout the world were likewise turned toward particularly brutal ends in Nazi Germany. For there, as in other countries, corporate control of massive numbers of workers was directed toward military activity. Nazi Germany's early efforts to overcome economic depression through the production of Volkswagens and the autobahn system were soon directed at mass producing armaments in factories that were patterned after the Ford car factories in the United States. These trucks, tanks, airplanes, and bombs were used against countries that Germany invaded, starting most dramatically with the invasion of Poland in 1939 and continuing with terrifying military exploits in Europe and North Africa that resulted in millions of deaths in World War II.

Perhaps the most disturbing modern industrial achievements of Nazi Germany were the numerous factories of death it built inside and outside of Germany. Probably the most infamous of these was Auschwitz, an extermination facility located in Poland that has become synonymous with the genocidal killing of Jews and other groups. In all there were six large-scale, mechanized installations in Poland, which included gas chambers, crematoriums for disposing of the bodies, and transportation systems to import huge numbers of victims. Such grim marvels of advanced engineering claimed the lives of millions of victims.

Different Fates

The Nazi drive for total control resulted in very different experiences for different groups inside Germany. In Germany of the 1930s and 1940s, the Nazi taste for unbridled governmental power was linked at its root to a hatred of outsiders. Sometimes such outsiders were defined in racial terms.

Early in their regime, the Nazis used modern concepts and methods to enact harmful, authoritarian measures against disabled people. They also targeted criminals, homosexuals, and political opponents such as Communists. People from these groups were the first to disappear in large numbers into Nazi prisons and concentration camps, without benefit of real (or any) trials or lawyers, as the Nazis engaged in sweeps and mass arrests of those seen as enemies of the state. The Germans had historic conflicts with Poland and Russia, so people from these nations were the objects of particular fury when Germany began its military aggression, took large numbers of prisoners, and treated them brutally.

The full use of modern, mechanized terror methods was unleashed against groups that the Nazis viewed as racially inferior, such as Jews and Gypsies. Gypsies had lived for many years on the fringes of German society. Jewish people, on the other hand, had been assimilated into Germany—a great many of them had converted to Christian religions or married non-Jews. Jews were also members of a variety of professions: They were store owners, teachers, and doctors. Still, there was strong sentiment against Jewish Germans among non-Jewish Germans, and Hitler did not make any secret of his hatred for Jews.

Neither Gypsies nor Jews comprised large groups—Jews made up only 0.8 percent of the German population. Nevertheless, the Nazis seized upon these groups, calling them enemies of Germany and—worse—claiming they were a race whose genes were polluting the bloodlines of real Germans, or Aryans, as the Nazis called them. Around 1935, two years after being named chancellor, Hitler announced laws that forbade Jews to have sex with non-Jewish Germans. Some married couples were forced to divorce. Members of the despised groups were at first forced to leave the country, often after being stripped of their bank accounts and other property.

In 1938 Jews began to be systematically rounded up and sent to concentration camps inside and outside of Germany. At the time, their fate was uncertain, although it was not uncommon for relatives left at home to receive urns containing the ashes of people who, it was claimed, had died of disease or been killed trying to escape from the camps.

In 1942, three years before Germany was defeated, a Nazi official made an announcement to a group of other officials about plans for the total liquidation of Jews. Although this announcement was not publicized, an unending stream of propaganda continued to depict Jews unfavorably. Jews and those of mixed heritage who were not yet in concentration camps were denied food rations, forced to live in special houses, and made to wear yellow stars on their sleeves in public.

"Ordinary" Germans

Germans who were not singled out for persecution fared better than members of groups designated as enemies. Hitler and the Nazi Party enjoyed massive popular support in Germany. Regular citizens attended rallies, watched parades, and eagerly listened to Hitler's speeches.

Nevertheless, it has been estimated that one hundred thousand Germans were killed for opposing the Nazis in one form or another. One person who was persecuted was Martin Niemöller, a German Protestant churchman. At first, he supported the Nazi Party. But after Hitler became chancellor in 1933, Niemöller preached courageously against the Hitler regime. He became a

16 Living in Nazi Germany

leader of the German pastors' emergency league. He was arrested in 1937 and again in 1938, when he was imprisoned until the end of World War II in 1945.

Many Germans found themselves in an uncertain status. For example, children of "mixed" marriages—who were designated *Mischling*, or "half-breeds"—were often exposed to harsh treatment. The following example vividly captures the terror of life under the Nazis: When Ilse Koehn was a schoolgirl, she wore a swastika and sang Hitler songs with her friends. She did not understand why her grandmother received ominous visits from officials.

Oma [grandmother] and I were eating when there was a sharp knock at the door, instantly followed by a staccato of louder, authoritative pounding. When I opened the door, I faced what seemed to be a gray wall moving toward me. I had the nightmare feeling that it would come close, closer, and crush me.

It consisted of two huge women dressed in long, identical gray coats....

"That must be her!" said one, pulling me up against her enormous body by one of my pigtails. She held it painfully tight, using her other hand to part the hair on my head this way and that. Then she released me with a push that made me stumble backward against Oma.

"At least she doesn't have lice!" she declared. "Is this the child?" she demanded of Oma as if she had caught her with stolen goods. But she did not wait for an answer. "We are social workers," she continued in that same tone. "We've come to see whether the child is being properly cared for."[5]

The old woman was eventually sent to a concentration camp where she died. But Ilse could not be told the truth until after the war: Her grandmother was Jewish.

The Elite

Even Germans who were associated with the powerful Nazi hierarchy could feel the harsh effects of the Nazi totalitarian urge. For example, Gertrude Weisker, the cousin of Hitler's girlfriend Eva Braun, complained that toward the end of the war, restrictions on travel within Germany meant that "with the Nazi regime we felt ourselves in a big concentration camp."[6]

"Aryan" Germans and Germans within the powerful Nazi ruling group, although they suffered from vicious infighting and a climate of suspicion, were in a much more favorable position than members of despised groups. Creative people, such as the architect Albert Speer and the filmmaker Leni Riefenstahl, have told of their happiness at using their party affiliations to get commissions to do Nazi-sponsored projects. Such commissions were all the more desirable during the economic depression that helped bring the Nazis to power.

Accounts of the Nazis' victims, ordinary Germans, and members of the Nazi hierarchy show that the Nazi quest for totalitarian power, although it was marked superficially by evidence of the modernity of the era, led at heart to extremes in the fates of different social groups within Germany. And if one goal of modernity is progress toward the achievement of a high quality of life for people of all classes, Nazi Germany can only be seen as a dismal failure and a step backward into a barbarian past.

Notes

1. Harold R. Kerbo and Hermann Strasser, *Modern Germany.* Boston: McGraw-Hill, 2000, p. ix.
2. Klaus P. Fischer, *Nazi Germany: A New History.* New York: Continuum, 1995, p. 294.
3. Fischer, *Nazi Germany*, pp. 370–71.
4. Quoted in Eileen Heyes, *Children of the Swastika.* Brookfield, CT: Millbrook, 1993, pp. 35–36.
5. Ilse Koehn, *Mischling, Second Degree: My Childhood in Nazi Germany.* New York: Greenwillow, 1977, pp. 22–23.
6. Quoted in Linda Grant, "My Cousin, Eva Braun," *Guardian* (London), April 27, 2002.

Life as a Target of Nazi Brutality

Chapter Preface

No government is more strongly associated with harsh treatment of its own citizens than Nazi Germany. But the brutal practices for which the era is remembered—death camps and the systematic murder of millions of people—did not come about overnight. It took the Nazis twelve years, from 1933 to 1945, to develop and refine the policies and put in place the supporting infrastructure—both physical and social—that would bring their violent goals to fruition.

Even in the 1920s and early 1930s, before he came to power, Adolf Hitler expressed vicious attitudes toward Jewish Germans and other groups such as Gypsies. Hitler expressed such beliefs in his book *Mein Kampf* and in his many speeches. Other party readers echoed these attitudes in newsletters and meetings.

In contrast to his disdain toward despised groups, Hitler promulgated a distorted love of "pure" German people, whom he called Aryans. The Nazis claimed the ideal Aryan had blonde hair, light eyes, and was physically fit—characteristics that, ironically, many prominent Nazi leaders did not themselves possess. (Hitler, for example, had dark coloration, not the ideal Aryan characteristics.)

Almost immediately after Hitler was appointed chancellor of Germany in 1933, Nazi leaders began sweeps and roundups of criminals and political opponents, creating an atmosphere of terror that gradually intensified throughout the era. The definition of a criminal became unclear. A criminal might be an alcoholic, a vagrant, someone who had unapproved sexual activities, a labor union leader, or a Communist Party member.

In the process of these arrests, the Nazis did not honor established legal principles such as the right to a trial and a lawyer. Thousands of Germans were subject to frequent arrest and long imprisonment during the Nazi years. Likewise, disabled people were involuntarily sterilized or even killed under the misnamed "euthanasia" policy.

There was little effective resistance to brutal Nazi policies from other citizens. This lack of response was probably due in large part to the fact that it soon became a grave crime, punishable by death, to even criticize Nazi policies. Moreover, many Germans, including Jewish Germans themselves, had difficulty believing that the Nazis would or could translate their venomous ideals into murderous policies. But gradually, despised groups lost their rights to hold many jobs, to marry outside their own group, to have money in the bank, or own real estate. Later, these people were denied the right to leave Germany and were forced to live in prescribed locations.

Then the roundups began to include people whose only "offense" was having the wrong religious or ethnic background. They began to be taken away en masse to camps in distant locations. While it was widely known that something bad was happening to such "deported" people, their fate was unclear until the early 1940s. The full horror of the death camps was not universally recognized until soldiers from the armies that vanquished Nazi Germany photographed the horrifying evidence in the liberated camps. From such evidence, it became clear that what had begun as a campaign of hatred against certain members of Germany's own citizenry had gradually developed into their large-scale destruction.

Police Justice

Robert Gellately

Immediately after Hitler's appointment as chancellor of Germany in 1933, the Nazis instituted dramatic changes to the justice system. The strong-arm methods they used to stifle crime and political dissent soon developed into a harsh crackdown on anybody who objected to their methods. The result was widespread arrests and atrocities such as concentration camps, which gave Nazi Germany its reputation as one of the most notorious criminal governments in history.

Robert Gellately is the Strassler Professor in Holocaust History at Clark University. In this excerpt, he describes how the Nazis exploited popular fears about crime to justify harsh police methods and the elimination of citizens' civil liberties.

The perception that Germany was falling apart during the Great Depression was reinforced by what seemed like a crime wave. Such perceptions were fuelled by the media, but the feeling that crime was increasing was not entirely without basis, for all across Germany, there was a steady climb for most years from 1927 to 1932 in thefts of all kinds, as well as in armed robbery and fraud. The rise was continuous in large cities (with 50,000 or more inhabitants), and some crimes nearly doubled between 1927 and 1932. In the last years of the Weimar Republic [the democratic federal government begun in 1919 after the country's defeat in World War I], newspapers were full of stories about crime, drugs, and murder, including the activities of organized gangs. There were many accounts of finance scandals, sexual predators, serial murderers, and even cannibalism. The emergence of gays and the growth of pornography were held up as evidence of depravity. The blossoming of unconventional styles in art and music made Berlin famous and drew freedom-loving souls from all around the world, where they celebrated their emancipation. It was just this kind of 'un-German' behaviour that many good citizens despised.

Robert Gellately, *Backing Hitler: Consent and Coercion in Nazi Germany*. New York: Oxford University Press, 2001. Copyright © 2001 by Robert Gellately. Reproduced by permission of the publisher.

The open society and democratic freedoms were new to Germany, and many people longed nostalgically for a more disciplined society of the kind they identified in their minds with the era before 1914. Many Germans, and not just those in the conservative, religious, or Nazi camps believed that the liberal Weimar Republic was a degenerate society, and that their country was on the road to ruin.

'The Fist Comes Down!'

Christopher Isherwood, the English novelist, wrote in 1933 just before leaving the free and easy Berlin he loved in the 1920s, that the newspapers were 'becoming more and more like copies of a school magazine. There is nothing in them but new rules, new punishments, and lists of people who have been "kept in"'. Law-abiding citizens, of course, saw matters differently, and could hardly fail to be pleased that police began to take seriously their concerns about crime and loose morals. One woman fondly recalled long after the Third Reich [the successor Hitler promised to two earlier empires] was gone, that even during the early years of the new regime, the laws were stiffened and supposedly even thieves were shot, so that thereafter 'nobody took anything that belonged to anyone else'.

The Nazi approach to crime was not to search out its deeper social causes, but to enforce existing laws far more vigorously. The Nazi motto was summed up in a front-page story of their leading newspaper in the phrase 'the fist comes down'. They adopted this stance even before the Reichstag [legislative body building] fire at the end of February 1933. They appointed new Police Presidents for a number of major cities, including Berlin, where hardliners promptly declared war on crime. The impression conveyed in the press was that the Nazi Party and the German police had a lot in common, as both hated Communism and were determined to stamp out crime.

Admiral von Levetzow, new head of the Berlin police, said he wanted to restore the tried-and-true German values embodied in his old-fashioned sounding name. In his address to uniformed police in mid-February 1933, he called on them to fight for 'law and order, for decency, for discipline and morality'. These were the mythical values associated with the strict Prussian past. At the end of March, Hitler demanded the 'purification of the body politic', and whatever that was supposed to mean in practical terms, the Nazis translated it into threats that criminals would now be treated with 'utmost severity'. The public was assured, as one headline put it, that prisoners behind bars would 'not continue to have it better than the unemployed'.

Preventive Arrest

In the early months of 1933, the police got temporary 'preventive' arrest powers to fight the Communists. These powers enabled the police to dispense with hearings before a judge and to hold Communists in what was called 'protective custody'. Until the Third Reich, protective custody was used in Germany to shield untried people from the wrath of the mob and keep them out of harm's way. Beginning in 1933, the meaning of 'protective custody' was turned on its head. It became a weapon in the hands of the Gestapo, a euphemism for their regular arrest and confinement practices. They could pick up men and women, send them to a concentration camp without trial, and keep them there indefinitely.

The Gestapo systematized their use of 'protective custody', anchored it in the exceptional measures decree at the end of February 1933, and never looked back. The system of 'police justice' was established at the expense of citizens' legal right. The Gestapo [Secret Police] used their new powers to track widely defined political crimes, and the Kripo [Criminal Police] obtained similar 'preventive arrest' powers to pursue other types of crimes. . . .

Law and Order

Law and order stories became constituent parts of Nazi mythology and were exaggerated. Nevertheless, the police were quick to use their new powers, even against petty thieves like exploiters and swindlers, who were packed off (without trials) to concentration camps. The same thing happened to butchers and cattle dealers who took advantage of the Depression to force farmers to sell livestock at low prices. Newspapers self-righteously declared that these criminals would now 'have an opportunity to discover through manual labour, how difficult the work of a farmer is and how much sweat and work it takes in these hard times to hold on to a bit of 'soil'. These stories about swift justice, undoubtedly fuelled populist myths about the regime as a crime fighter, and thus earned it considerable support.

In September 1933, using imagery drawn from the military, the police declared open war on the beggars and vagrants. Citizens were discouraged from showing false pity, and asked to give their money instead to charities. A police sweep across the country picked up as many as 100,000 and as a recent study puts it, 'never before had the police in Germany taken in so many people by way of a single police action.'

In the days and weeks that followed, the press was full of glowing stories about the event, like one that proudly proclaimed 'Berlin, a City without beggars'. In December another featured a 'Report on the Cleansing of Berlin' stating that 'the measures of the Berlin police and their results find the support of everyone. The capital city is freed within a few months from an evil whose scale represented an unacceptable annoyance to Berliners and to visitors in the city.'

The beginning of better times and diminished crime was signalled in a Christmas-time story that ran under the headline, 'Insecurity Diminished: there is work again for the people; now we can go home again at night in peace.' Although some of the beggars who were arrested were soon released, the no-nonsense image of the new system was hammered home in the press. In Hamburg the police took the opportunity not only to arrest beggars, but to force unemployed single men and others to work for any welfare support they received. There was a crackdown on petty criminals, like those who lived from the avails of prostitution. On 24 November 1933, the penalty for this crime was drastically increased, from a minimum of one month (in less onerous-style prison or workhouse) to a minimum of five years in the hardest form of it.

Almost immediately after Hitler's appointment, the impression in the press was that at the very least, more use would be made of the death penalty and it would be carried out sooner after sentencing than in the past. There were also menacing announcements that capital punishment could be used for 'violations' of measures adopted by the new government.

New Criminal Code

Discussions about making the method of execution uniform across Germany—whether it should be hanging, shooting, the executioner's axe, or the guillotine—were taken up by a commission formed to give Germany a new Criminal Code. Hitler considered the idea of changing the Criminal Code, whose weaknesses he never tired of pointing out. . . .

Hitler . . . preferred a system in which the police not only enforced existing or written law, but decided what the law was. Those who favoured 'police justice' did not want the police restricted in any way. . . .

The many reports over the years, even if unwittingly, suggested to the public that the liberal legal system was hopelessly weak on crime. In place of the outmoded Weimar system, commissioners favoured one that reflected 'racial values' and fostered the 'community of the people'. They wanted to demolish equality before the law, the essence of the liberal legal order, and in its place make legal rights contingent on the extent to which the accused person was a useful member of society. They favoured speedier trials and the reduction of legal protections for the accused and they wanted to count an attempted (but failed) crime as equivalent to one that succeeded. They also wanted to Nazify certain old crimes, for example, by supplementing the traditional concept of 'treason against the state' by adding 'treason against the race'. They wanted to make it possible for judges to punish someone who offended 'wholesome popular sentiment', even though they might not have broken a law. Whereas the old law code supposedly favoured the 'security of the criminal', the new one aimed at 'securing the community of the people.'

No Crime Without Punishment

Citizens were told that the liberal principle of 'no crime without a law' (*nullum crimen sine lege*), was changed into 'no crime without a punishment' (*nullum crimen sine poena*). This slogan was meant to appeal to those fed up that the justice system gave too many rights to perpetrators of crime and ignored the social costs. The catchy Latin phrase was translated and popularized in the press, and as early as mid-1934 was even reprinted on small postage-stamp posters that were glued to the covers of court dossiers. Presumably the little stamp would inspire the everyday activities of lawyers and judges in the courts, and it read as follows: 'Then: [that is, before 1933] No punishment without law. Now: No crime without punishment.'

Hitler's statement on such legal changes was very simple. He said on the fourth anniversary of his appointment, noticeably leaving out any mention of the emergency that was supposedly justified by a Communist threat, that 'the mission of the justice system is to contribute to the preservation and the securing of the volk [people, nation] in the face of certain elements who, as asocials [criminals, undesirables], strive to avoid common duties or who sin against these common interests. Thus, the volk takes precedence over persons and property, also in German law.'

Once Hitler's new police got a taste for speedy measures, however, by which they could bypass time-consuming legal procedures, there was no chance they were ever really going to dispense with them. In mid-1934 they got an opportunity to bid for public support, when they finally came down on the Storm Troopers (SA). On 30 June 1934, the leaders of the SA were killed on Hitler's orders. During this so-called 'night of the long knives' the radical ambitions of the SA, who kept longing for a real social revolution, were brought to a halt once and for all. The event was presented to the German public as an attempted coup by SA leader Ernst Röhm, but no effort was made to hide the fact that Röhm was executed without a semblance of a trial. Most people accepted that Hitler (not the courts) 'sentenced' the 100 or so culprits to death. Far from causing Germans to have second thoughts, by all accounts this first mass murder of the Third Reich paid positive political dividends for Hitler, because it gave many citizens the opportunity to accept the new 'normality' and the coercive side of the dictatorship. The police wanted the government to be more trusting than to censor news and to be upfront about what happened to those killed during the purge. They felt it was impossible to stop citizens from listening to foreign radio, and suggested it would be best to publish 'authentic explanations to remove the basis of wild rumours'.

Hitler signalled that political stabilization had arrived by granting a selective amnesty on 10 August 1934. He used the occasion of President Hindenburg's death and opportunity to publicize the 'unification of the office of Reich President with that of the Reich Chancellor'. The amnesty was supposed to still the worries of top civil servants and to assure the general population that all was well, in spite of what was called the Röhm 'revolt'. According to press reports, as many as one-third of those in 'protective custody' were released in some places, and more concentration camps were dissolved. The reports stated that 'deadly enemies' who prepared and carried out acts of treason were not included in the amnesty, but that many already had left the country.

Hitler was not interested in legal niceties, so it was characteristic that he did not disband the Gestapo, nor curtail its powers, even though most of those considered real enemies were by that time already gone. On the contrary, on 20 June 1935, he gave Himmler his blessing to expand the concentration camps, which had been closing down everywhere. Himmler also obtained Hitler's support on 18 October 1935 to broaden the powers of the police. A meeting between them took place shortly after the infamous Nuremberg Party rally in September at which Hitler announced discriminatory laws against the Jews.

Expanding Persecution

The Nuremberg rally in 1935, heralded as the 'National Party Meeting of Freedom', represented a milestone in the establishment of the dictatorship's system of racial discrimination and persecution. Of three new laws passed on 15 September by the Reichstag [legislative body] which met in Nuremberg, the most important turned out to be the 'law for the protection of German blood and German honour'. The law forbad further marriages and extramarital sexual relations between Jews and 'Germans' and people of 'associated or similar blood'.

Another part of the Nuremberg event, one frequently overlooked, took place on 11 September, when Hitler announced by proclamation what he termed a 'struggle against the internal enemies of the nation'. These 'enemies' were vaguely defined as 'Jewish Marxism and the parliamentary democracy associated with it'; 'the politically and morally depraved Catholic Centre Party'; and 'certain elements of an unteachable, dumb and reactionary bourgeoisie'. The proclamation did not say what steps would be taken, but it sounded like the beginning of a social war.

The speech was all the more curious in that it went on to underline how Germany enjoyed greater security and tranquillity than at any time in the recent past. Hitler contrasted the situation in 1935 with the 'ferment of decomposition' and 'signs of decay' that existed at the time of his appointment.

A little over a month after the Nuremberg rally, on 18 October 1935 Hitler and Himmler broadened the concepts of 'enemy' and 'crime' the new police were supposed to fight. The Gestapo was not going to vanish after all, nor were the camps. The number of camp prisoners had been falling since mid-1933, but promptly began to grow again.

By mid-1935 the new police were getting the upper hand. At this time the dictatorship had to respond to the issue of whether suspects in protective custody should be allowed legal counsel. The argument as stated by Dr Werner Best, a key figure behind the creation of the new system, was simple. The main consideration 'from the point of view of the leadership of the state', he said, was whether or not giving lawyers access to clients would help in the battle against the state's 'deadly enemies'. Lawyers' questions were inevitable, but were incompatible with the state leadership's 'trust in the organizations given the mission to defend against the attacks of enemies'. Best said that because the Gestapo regarded protective custody as its 'most important weapon against enemies of state, any weakening of that weapon was the equivalent of strengthening the dangers threatening the state. Therefore, he concluded, no lawyers should be allowed as the usual 'procedural forms of the judiciary were totally inapplicable for the struggle against the enemies of state under the present circumstances'. That argument was met by a minor quibble from the Ministry of Justice, which was silenced when Himmler informed officials on 6 November 1935 of a Hitler order barring lawyers access to anyone held in protective custody.

The Völkisch Police

The creation of the new Gestapo system culminated with a Prussian law of 10 February 1936. According to this law virtually any actions taken by the Gestapo were no longer subject to court review, not even in the event of wrongful arrest, and no one could sue for damages. In other words, if the Gestapo was above the law even earlier, by early 1936 that situation was formalized. Henceforth, the only route open for any complaints was to appeal to the Gestapo head office (Gestapa). Far from being hushed up, the full implications of these developments were spelled out to the public in the press, so that no doubt could exist that citizens' basic legal rights were all but ended. Gestapo headquarters in Berlin simply wished to ensure that local officials did not overuse their powers of arrest and bring discredit on the police. Although in theory the legal immunity enjoyed by the Gestapo did not apply to the rest of the police, if and when they acted on behalf of the Gestapo, what they did could not be challenged either.

The Nazis worked out a clearly articulated *völkisch* or Fascist theory of the police by the mid-1930s, and proudly presented it for the edification and enlightenment of the public. The most succinct statement of this new theory was by Werner Best, the legal expert at Gestapo headquarters. Although his remarks were published in a specialist journal, summaries of them made their way into the popular press. Germans could now read that the police powers justified initially to fight Communism had a new rationale. Best stated flatly that the new police regarded 'every attempt' to realize or to maintain any political theory besides National Socialism 'as a symptom of sickness, which threatens the healthy unity of the indivisible volk organism'. All such efforts would be 'eliminated regardless of the subjective intentions of their proponents'. He now said that the new police watched over the 'health of the German body politic', recognized 'every system of sickness', and destroyed all 'destructive cells'. He summed up the mission of the Gestapo as follows:

> The preventive police mission of a political police is to search out the enemies of state, to watch them and at the right moment to destroy them. In order to fulfil this mission the political police must be free to use every means required to achieve the necessary goal. In the National Socialist leader state it is the case, that those institutions called upon to protect state and people to carry out the will of the state, possess as of right the complete authority required to fulfil their task, an authority that derives solely from the new conception of the state and one that requires no special legal legitimization.

Best used the comparison between the Gestapo and the army

at war, when he wrote that the Gestapo 'in its struggle against clever, determined and ruthless enemies must claim the same trust and the same powers as an army, which in fulfilment of its task—to destroy an enemy whose behaviour cannot be predicted—also cannot be bound by the letter of the law'. What had to be recognized about the police and the law, according to Best, was that above all 'for the fulfilment of its tasks, which could not be mastered according to fixed norms, the police must be given the same authority to take the necessary measures on the basis of its own knowledge and own responsibility so as to ensure the security of the people and state'.

This kind of *völkisch* or biological theory of the police was presented to the German people as the rational basis for what the new police did. Himmler reported calmly in March 1937 that the tradition of the nightwatchman state was dead, and so was the old liberal order in which, theoretically at least, the police were neutral. Whereas the old police watched but did not interfere to fulfil agendas of their own, the new police, he said, were no longer subject to any formal restrictions in carrying out their mission, which included enforcing the will of the leadership and creating and defending the kind of social order it desired.

According to Reichsminister Hans Frank, it was unthinkable for police to be restricted merely to maintaining law and order. He said that these concepts used to be considered value-free and neutral, but in Hitler's dictatorship, 'philosophical neutrality no longer exists', that is, supporting or embracing any other political view besides Nazism was a crime. For the new police, the priority was 'the protection and advancement of the community of the people', and police counter-measures were justified against every 'agitation' opposed to the people, and had to 'smother' them. The police could take whatever steps were necessary, including the invasion of house and home, 'because there exists no private sphere any more, in which the individual is permitted to work unmolested at the destruction of the basis of the National Socialist community's life'.

Living in a Concentration Camp

Eugene Kogon

Nazi Germany created numerous concentration camps for political opponents, criminals, and groups deemed "inferior"—including Jews, Gypsies, and homosexuals. The trend started in 1933 with fifty "work" camps within Germany. By the time World War II ended, the number, size and harshness of the camps had increased and they had spread around Europe. An infamous example is Auschwitz, in Poland, a death camp designed to kill people efficiently; some estimate that 4.5 million perished there.

Eugene Kogon was taken prisoner for his anti-Nazi activities in 1938. He was finally freed in 1945, when the camp at Buchenwald was liberated. Due to his long captivity as a political prisoner and his background in sociology, Kogon was asked by a U.S. team to write a report on the camps for trials and intelligence purposes. The report was eventually made into a book, from which this selection is taken. In it, Kogon vividly describes the oppressive living conditions, the abuse, and the constant terror camp inmates endured.

The camp was awakened by whistles, in the summer between four and five o'clock, in the winter between six and seven o'clock. Half an hour was allotted to washing, dressing, breakfasting and bed-making, sometimes an impossible job within that period.

A number of camps insisted on morning calisthenics, performed winter and summer at break-neck pace for half an hour before the regular rising time. They consisted mostly of everlasting push-ups in the snow and muck. Because of numerous fatal cases of pneumonia, this practice never persisted for very long.

Breakfast consisted of a piece of bread from the ration issued for the day and a pint of thin soup or so-called "coffee," without

---

Eugene Kogon, *The Theory and Practice of Hell*. New York: Berkley Books, 1998.

either milk or sugar. The bread ration was issued at different times to different barracks. Those who had got it at night and had immediately eaten it up had no bread for breakfast.

Next came morning roll call. On a signal the prisoners from each barracks fell in on the camp street and marched eight abreast to the roll-call area. Thousands of zebra-striped figures of misery, marching under the glare of the floodlights in the haze of dawn, column after column—no one who has even witnessed it is likely to forget the sight.

Each barracks had its own assigned place in the roll-call area. The entire strength of the camp was counted, and this roll call usually took an hour, until it was light enough to start work. Morning roll call was not as important as its evening counterpart, still to be discussed, for little change was likely to take place overnight—deaths during the night were reported ahead of time from the prisoner hospital. After roll call came a thunderous command from the Roll Call Officer over the public-address system, addressed to the army of shorn men: "Caps off!" and "Caps on!" This was the morning salute for the Officer-in-Charge. If it was not executed smartly enough, it had to be repeated again and again, to the accompaniment of such comment as this: "You god-damned ass-holes, if you're too lazy to ventilate your filthy pates, I'll make you practice till the juice boils in your tails, you sons of bitches!"

A Stab in the Heart

Now came the dreaded call: "Prisoners under orders to the gatehouse!" It affected all those who had received a slip from the Orderly Room the night before. In Buchenwald six numbered signs were mounted at the wall of the left wing of the gatehouse. There the prisoners had to await the nameless terror about to engulf them. When they had painfully come to learn which number meant a summons before the Political Department, and which indicated more harmless matters—records, signatures, notarizations, etc—the assignment of the numbers would be suddenly changed. The prisoners often had to wait for hours, haunted by uncertainty. If their families had only known the fear they could engender by routine inquiries and business matters! It was impossible to evade such a summons, and the waiting prisoners were at the mercy of the SS [security police] men who always loitered near the gatehouse.

Often prisoners so summoned were not given notice the night before at all. Their numbers were simply called out at the end of morning roll call and they were ordered to report to such-and-such a sign. I can state from personal experience that such an unexpected announcement of one's number was like a stab in the heart, regardless of what was involved.

The next command was "Labor details—fall in!" There was a wild milling about, as the prisoners moved to their assigned assembly points with all possible speed. The camp band, in the winter-time scarcely able to move its fingers, played merry tunes as the columns moved out five abreast. At the gatehouse caps had to be snatched off again, hands placed at the trouser seams. The details then marched off in double time, the prisoners compelled to sing.

Work continued until late afternoon, with half an hour for lunch, out in the open. For a long time the prisoners were not permitted to carry bread with them. Under an alternate plan, the details marched back into camp at noon, for half an hour or three-quarters, to bolt down their lunch. This hot meal, the only one all day, generally consisted of a single dish—a quart of soup or broth, often very thin and devoid of nourishment. The work schedule differed from camp to camp, but by and large it followed the schemes here described.

Evening Terrors

In the winter work ended around five o'clock, in the summer, around eight—between March and November the time was periodically shifted by half-hour intervals. At the conclusion of the work day the prisoners were marched back to camp, past the band, again ordered to play sprightly tunes. Then came evening roll call.

In every camp this head count was the terror of the prisoners. After a hard day's work, when ordinary men look forward to well-deserved rest, they had to stand in ranks for hours on end, regardless of rain or storm or icy cold, until the SS had tallied its slaves and established that none had escaped during the day. The preliminary work for these roll calls often had to be done by prisoner clerks, since few SS men were capable of making an accurate tabulation. The prisoners always endeavored to avoid the slightest error, especially in counting the numerous inmates on "permanent detail," whose work brooked no interruption and who therefore never appeared in line, though they were, of course, counted. Any slip, even though not a man was missing, was likely to result in hours of checking and delay, depriving the exhausted prisoners of the last shreds of leisure. So long as the number of prisoners to be accounted for did not exceed 5,000 to 7,000, any absence was quickly noted. It was a different matter when the number swelled to 20,000, to say nothing of 50,000. A great many non-German inmates looked on this roll call as just another form of Prussian drill, to be evaded whenever possible. On many occasions a shirker would simply sleep away roll call in some hiding place, while tens of thousands of his fellows stood in stupor and agony until the culprit was found. (His would be an unenviable lot—no one took pity on him!) If a single prisoner was absent, hundreds of names and numbers from various barracks had to be called out—Polish names, Russian names, French names that could be pronounced only with the aid of interpreters. The SS men would lose their tempers, bellow, and let their fists and boots fly. Few roll calls took less than an hour and a half.

Escapes

Whenever a prisoner actually escaped, the whole camp was kept on its feet until he was recaptured, often a matter of many hours. Guards were kept posted around the entire camp area during roll call, to insure that no prisoner could lurk about the headquarters area. The search within this guard line was the job of the Senior Block Inmates, the Barracks Orderlies, the Prisoner Foremen and the Camp Police. Successful escapes drew such savage punishment upon the entire camp, especially in the early years, that the political prisoners renounced even the attempt until the final months. Then a few escapes, undertaken with the approval of the underground leadership, proved necessary in order to establish contact with the approaching Allies.

During evening roll call on December 14, 1938, two convicts turned up missing at Buchenwald. The temperature was 5° above zero and the prisoners were thinly clad—but they had to stand in the roll-call area for nineteen hours. Twenty-five had frozen to death by morning; by noon the number had risen to more than seventy.

During the fall of 1939 there was another occasion when the entire camp was kept standing for eighteen hours on end, because two convicts had hidden in the pigsty. Oh, it is easy enough to write about now—standing like that, after a full day's work, throughout the night and until next noon, without food! The cold death figures can be set down—but not the permanent damage suffered by hundreds who later perished of the after effects. What a relief when the war in the air forced even the SS to black out, when the floodlights could no longer be turned on! From that time onward, roll call simply had to be called off after a certain period, whether there were any absences or not. In the complete blackout the SS would have lost control of the camp, would have had good reason for fear in its own ranks.

From time to time the Block Leaders were ordered to "frisk" the inmates during roll call. Pockets had to be emptied and the contents were examined by the SS, a process during which as a

Starved prisoners pose at a concentration camp in Austria

rule much money and tobacco simply disappeared. One Sunday in February (!) 1938, the prisoners were compelled to stand stripped to the skin for three hours on such an occasion. The wife of Commandant Koch, in company with the wives of four other SS officers, came to the wire fence to gloat at the sight of the naked figures.

Roll call was a time for many special tortures. Often, following the head count, the command would be heard, "All Jews, remain behind"—to sing over and over again deep into the night the vile jingles known as the "Jew song":

> For years we wreaked deceit upon the nation,
> No fraud too great for us, no scheme too dark,
> All that we did was cheat and lie and swindle,
> Whether with dollar or with pound or mark.

It ended with the following verses:

> But now at last the Germans know our nature
> And barbed wire hides us safely out of sight.
> Traducers of the people, we were fearful
> To face the truth that felled us overnight.
>
> And now, with mournful crooked Jewish noses,
> We find that hate and discord were in vain.
> An end to thievery, to food aplenty.
> Too late, we say, again and yet again.

This choice product of Nazi culture was the work of one of the "asocials" who sought to insinuate himself into the favor of the SS. Rodl, a man who could hardly be described as very discriminating, had the Jews sing it twice and then even he had enough. He forbade it. It was Officers-in-Charge Florstedt and Plaul, vicious anti-Semites, who restored it to Nazi honors. An especially popular procedure for entertaining visitors to the camps was to have the Jews line up in the roll-call area to the left of the tower and sing the vile tune.

Alive or Dead

Everyone had to appear for roll call, whether alive or dead, whether shaken by fever or beaten to a bloody pulp. The only exceptions were inmates on permanent detail, and those in the prisoner hospital. The bodies of men who had died during the day, either in the barracks or at work, had to be dragged to the roll-call area. During particularly virulent sieges, there were always dozens of dying and dead laid in neat "rank and file" beyond the block formations, to answer the final roll call. For the SS exacted order and discipline down to the last breath. Not until after roll call could the dying be taken to the hospital, the dead to the morgue.

Once evening roll call was over, with the commands of "Caps off!" and "Caps on!" there usually followed another command: "Left face!"—and the public punishments . . . were meted out. Or one of the Officers-in-Charge might call for a song. It might be raining or storming. The prisoners might scarcely be able to keep to their feet. All the more reason for exacting a song, as much as possible at odds with the situation—once, three times, five times in succession—"I saw a little bird flying," or "Something stirs in the forest." Most of the camps had songs of their own, written and composed by prisoners, on command. Some of these have become widely known, notably "The Peat-Bog Soldiers" and "The Buchenwald Song."

It might have been thought that once the final "Fall out!" had sounded the day's torments were over and the prisoners could sit down to eat and rest at leisure. But often they returned to the barracks, only to be confronted by the results of the inspections conducted during the day by the Block Leaders—lockers overturned, their contents scattered in every direction. The search for one's mess kit often led to savage clashes among the prisoners, driven beyond the limits of human endurance.

When the prisoners worked through the day, the main meal was issued at night. Of course it was cold by the time a protracted roll call was completed. The remaining ration, when issued at night, consisted of bread, a dab of margarine, and a bit of sausage or possibly a spoonful of cottage cheese. At any moment during "dinner" the Barracks Orderly might suddenly sing out: "Attention! B-wing of Barrack X reporting! One hundred and thirty-five prisoners at mess!" Some SS sergeant had conceived the notion to pay a visit. Not yet through the door, he would bellow: "Get under the tables, you swine!" Benches would be overturned, mess gear clatter to the floor. Still, there were always a few left over who, try as they might, could not find room under the tables and became the particular whipping boys. There were many variations on this tune. A Block Leader might simply order a barracks cleared during the meal, having the prisoners execute some senseless command, such as standing on their heads in the snow. To execute a headstand is not the easiest thing, even for a youngster. But even the aged and decrepit had to do it as a matter of course, just as they might have to double-time endlessly around the barracks. Any hesitation drew kicks and beatings. Even when nothing whatever happened in the barracks after roll call, the prisoners were obsessed by the fear that lightning might strike at any moment.

Sleep

If roll call had been concluded with reasonable dispatch, work had to be continued for several hours deep into the night by certain prisoner groups. The rest might stroll about the camp streets, in front of the barracks, in the washrooms or toilets—unless they preferred to retire immediately. When taps sounded—between eight and ten o'clock, according to season—everyone except those on detail had to be indoors, half an hour later in bed.

Prisoners were permitted to wear only their shirts while sleeping, even in the deep of winter, when the barracks grew bitter cold and the damp stone walls often coated with ice at the windows and corners. Block Leaders frequently conducted night inspections, ordering all the inmates in a barracks to line up beside the beds or even outdoors, in order to catch those who might be wearing an additional garment. Whoever was found in socks or underwear could expect merciless punishment. On occasion an entire barracks was chased around the block for as much as an hour, barefoot and dressed only in shirts.

These nocturnal invasions did not occur regularly. They came from time to time, at irregular intervals, unexpectedly, generally when the Block Leaders were drunk. But they *could* happen at any moment. The threat was ever-present. Mercifully, the prisoners were far too exhausted to brood on the danger. For a few short hours each night sleep spread its balm over the misery. Only the aged, the fretful, the sick, the sleepless, lay awake in a torment of worry, awaiting the ordeal of another day.

Growing Up Black in Nazi Germany

Hans Massaquoi

Young Hans Massaquoi was in a unique situation in Nazi Germany as the son of a well-to-do African father and a white German mother. Because of Hans's frail health, he and his mother stayed in Germany when his father and grandfather returned to Liberia in 1929. When the Nazi party came to power, Hans was too young to realize that, like everyone who was not of the "master" Aryan race, he was in danger. Like other boys at his school, he yearned to join the Hitler Youth and participate in other youth activities heavily promoted by the party. His realization that he was different and that the difference was a major threat to his well-being was at times shocking. This selection tells the story of one of Hans's early and most painful experiences, when he was rejected by the junior division of the Hitler Youth. In the 1950s, Massaquoi moved to the United States, where he joined the U.S. Army and became a journalist and managing editor of *Ebony* magazine.

Not long after his rise to power, Hitler let it be known that those diehards who refused to embrace his Nazi ideology were part of the old order that was on the way out. Regardless of the parents' political persuasion, he boasted, he would make sure to have the undying devotion and loyalty of their sons and daughters. "Germany's youth," he bragged, "will belong to me."

To make good on his boast, schools throughout Germany were ordered to mount elaborate drives aimed at recruiting pupils for the *Hitlerjugend* (HJ)—the Hitler Youth movement. The schools were aided in their efforts by a formidable arsenal of visual aids—charts, slides, documentary and feature films—churned out by [Paul Joseph] Goebbels's propaganda ministry, which spared no effort when it came to winning converts among the young. One

---

Hans Massaquoi, *Destined to Witness—Growing Up Black in Nazi Germany*. New York: William Morrow and Company, Inc., 1999. Copyright © 1999 by Hans J. Massaquoi. All rights reserved. Reproduced by permission of HarperCollins Publishers.

such film, *Hitlerjunge Quecks*, left a lasting impression on me when it was screened in my school during *Volkskunde* (folklore) class. It was the tragic story of a handsome, blond teenage boy nicknamed Quecks, who grows up in a predominantly Communist Berlin slum. His father, an alcoholic Communist sympathizer, who divides his time between getting drunk and mistreating his wife, was played convincingly by Heinrich George, at the time Germany's premier character actor and an avowed Hitler fan.

Escaping temporarily from his seamy surroundings, Quecks secretly attends a Hitler Youth outing where, within an idyllic Boy Scout-like setting, he experiences for the first time in his life wholesome camaraderie and bonding around a campfire. When he returns to his bleak neighborhood, he does so as a converted *Hitlerjunge* and active worker for the Nazi cause. While distributing Nazi leaflets, Quecks is cornered by one of his father's Communist cronies, who, after branding him a traitor, knifes him to death. As Quecks lies dying in the arms of his new Nazi comrades to the strains of the Hitler Youth's anthem, "*Vorwärts, Vorwärts* (Forward, Forward)," composed by no less a Nazi honcho than HJ leader Baldur von Schirach himself, he becomes the youngest martyr of the movement.

The film left as deep an impression on my ten-year-old, impressionable, non-Aryan mind as it did on the minds of my Aryan peers. I know, because when after the movie the window shades were raised, there was a suspicious rash of nose-blowing and sniffles throughout the auditorium.

Recruitment Drive

It would be years before I discovered that the film's message of Nazi virtue and Communist evil had been a brazen distortion of the facts. The truth was that during their many bloody clashes for dominance in Germany, the Nazis and Commies were virtually indistinguishable. Both were totalitarians, ever ready to brutalize in order to crush resistance to their respective ideologies.

With arch-Nazi [school principal] Wriede at the helm, Kätnerkampschule [Hans's school] aggressively pursued the indoctrination and recruitment of young souls for the *Jungvolk*, the HJ's junior league for ten- to thirteen-year-olds, whose members were known as *Pimpfe* (cubs). Hardly a day went by without our being reminded by our teachers or Wriede himself that for a German boy, life outside the movement was no life at all. Pursuing his objective with characteristic single-mindedness, Wriede was tireless in thinking up new gimmicks to further his goal. One day, he announced his latest brainchild, a schoolwide contest in which the first class to reach 100 percent *Jungvolk* membership would be rewarded with a holiday.

The immediate effect of the announcement was that my new homeroom teacher Herr Schürmann became obsessed with the idea of winning the coveted prize for our class and some brownie points for himself. Toward that end, he became a veritable pitchman, who spent much of his—and our—time trying to persuade, cajole, or otherwise induce our class to join the Nazi fold. The centerpiece of his recruitment drive was a large chart he had carefully drawn on the blackboard with white chalk. It consisted of a large box divided into as many squares as there were boys in the class. Each morning, Herr Schürmann would inquire who had joined the Hitler Youth. After a show of hands, he would count them, then gleefully add the new enlistees' names to his chart. Gradually the squares with names increased until they outnumbered the blank ones.

Up to that point I had followed the contest with a certain degree of emotional detachment because quite a few of my classmates, including some of my closest pals, had let it be known that they had no interest in anything the HJ did and would not join, no matter what Wriede or Schürmann had to say. That suited me fine since I, too, had no intention of joining. But under the relentless pressure from Schürmann, one resister after another caved in and joined.

A Bolt of Lightning

One morning, when the empty squares had dwindled to just a few, Herr Schürmann started querying the holdouts as to the reasons for their "lack of love for Führer and *Vaterland* [fatherland]." Some explained that they had nothing against Führer and *Vaterland* but weren't particularly interested in the kinds of things the *Jungvolk* were doing, such as camping, marching, blowing bugles and fanfares, and beating on medieval-style drums. Others said they didn't have their parents' permission, whereupon Herr

Schürmann instructed them to bring their parents in for a conference. When it came to what I thought was my turn to explain, I opened my mouth, but Herr Shürmann cut me off. "That's all right; you are exempted from the contest since you are ineligible to join the *Jungvolk*."

The teacher's words struck me like a bolt of lightning. Not eligible to join? What was he talking about? I had been prepared to tell him that I hadn't quite made up my mind whether I wanted to join or not. Now he was telling me that, even if I wanted to, I couldn't. Noticing my bewildered expression, Herr Schürmann told me to see him immediately after class.

Until the bell rang, I remained in a state of shock, unable to follow anything that was said. I felt betrayed and abandoned by my friends and terrified at the prospect of being the only person in class whose name would not appear on the chart. At age ten, I was as tough as any of my peers, able to take just about anything they dished out in the course of rough-and-tumble schoolboy play. What I couldn't take, however, was feeling that I didn't belong—being treated like an outcast, being told, in effect, that I was not only different but inferior.

Schürmann invited me to take a seat beside his desk. "I always thought you knew that you could not join the *Jungvolk* because you are non-Aryan," he began. "You know your father is an African. Under the Nuremberg Laws, non-Aryans are not allowed to become members of the Hitler Youth movement." Charitably, perhaps to spare at least some of my feelings, he omitted the much maligned and despised Jews from his roster of ineligibles.

"But I am a German," I sobbed, my eyes filling with tears. "My mother says I'm German just like anybody else."

"You *are* a German boy," Herr Schürmann conceded with unusual compassion, "but unfortunately not quite like anybody else."

Having gotten his point only too well, I made no further plea.

"I'm very sorry, my boy," Schürmann concluded the conference. "I wish I could help you, but there's nothing I can do; it's the law."

Quest for Acceptance

That evening, when I saw my mother, I didn't tell her what had transpired in school. Instead, I asked her to come with me to the nearest *Jungvolk Heim*, the neighborhood *Jungvolk* den just one block up the street, so I could join. Since I had never expressed the slightest interest in joining the HJ, she had never felt it necessary to burden me with the thought that I would be rejected. Thus, my sudden decision to join took her completely by surprise. When she tried to talk me out of it, even hinting that there was a possibility of my not being accepted, I grew frantic. I told her that I simply had to join since I could not be the only one in my class who was not an HJ member. But she still didn't think it was a good idea. "Please take me," I pleaded, almost hysterically. "Maybe they'll make an exception. Please!"

Against her better judgment, my mother finally relented and agreed to do whatever she could to help me join. When we arrived at the HJ *Heim*, a long, solidly built, one-story stone structure, the place was buzzing with activities and paramilitary commandos. Through the open door of a classroomlike meeting room, I could see a group of boys, most of them about my age, huddled around a long table, apparently listening to a troop leader's lecture. They wore neat uniforms, black shorts, black tunics over khaki shirts, and black scarfs that were held together at the neck by braided leather knots. Most of them, I noticed with envy, wore the small black *Dolch* (dagger) with the rhombus-shaped swastika emblem of the Hitler Youth. Ever since seeing it displayed in the window of a neighborhood uniform store, I had secretly coveted this largely ceremonial weapon. Even the words *Blut and Ehre* (blood and honor) that were engraved on its shiny blade, and whose symbolic meaning had totally eluded me, stirred my soul. I knew that once my membership in the HJ had been approved, nothing would stand in the way of my becoming a proud owner of a Hitler Youth *Dolch*. I wanted it so much, I could almost feel it in my hand.

"Snickers and Giggles"

After one *Pimpf* spotted me, I immediately became the subject of snickers and giggles until the troop leader, annoyed by the distraction, shouted *"Ruhe* (Quiet)!" and closed the door. When my mother asked a passing *Pimpf* to show us to the person in charge, he clicked his heels, then pointed to a door with the sign HEIMFÜRER. Upon my mother's knock, a penetrating male voice shouted, "Enter!"

"*Heil Hitler!* What can I do for you?" asked the handsome, roughly twenty-year-old man in the uniform of a mid-level Hitler Youth leader who was seated behind a desk. He reminded me of an older version of my erstwhile bodyguard, Wolfgang, tall, athletic, blond, and blue eyed—in short, Hitler's ideal Aryan man.

My mother returned the mandatory Nazi salute, then asked, "Is this the right place to apply for membership?"

The young man looked incredulous. "Membership for whom? For *him*?" he inquired, his eyes studying me as if they had spied a repulsive worm.

"Yes, for my son," my mother responded without flinching.

The Nazi recoiled. "I must ask you to leave at once," he commanded. "Since it hasn't occurred to you by now, I have to tell you that there is no place for your son in this organization or in the Germany we are about to build. *Heil Hitler!*" Having said that, he rose and pointedly opened the door.

For a moment I thought my mother would strike the man with her fist. She was trembling and glaring at him with an anger I had never before seen in her eyes. But she quickly regained her composure, took me by the hand, and calmly said, "Let's go." Neither she nor I spoke a word on the way back home. I felt guilty for having been the cause of her anguish and humiliation, and I was afraid she would be angry. Instead, when we reached our apartment, she just hugged me and cried. "I'm so sorry, I'm so sorry" was all she could say.

Seeing my mother like this was more than I could bear. "Please don't cry, Mutti," I pleaded while tears were streaming down my cheeks. It was a rare occurrence, since usually we outdid each other in keeping our hurt to ourselves. We were Germans, after all.

Erased

Two days later, the moment I had dreaded with ever-mounting anguish arrived. Herr Schürmann, with a joyfulness bordering on ecstasy, chalked in the final two names on his chart. He then took a wet sponge and carefully erased the last remaining empty square, the one that represented me, thereby graphically emphasizing my non-person status. "Congratulations, class! We have just reached our goal of one hundred percent HJ membership," he rejoiced. "I am extremely proud of you and grateful that you have brought honor to your class and to me. I think we should let the principal in on the good news." With that, he left the classroom, only to return a few minutes later with Wriede in tow.

The principal praised the class for having "dedicated your lives to Adolf Hitler and his vision of the Third Reich." Since it was a Saturday and therefore only a half school day, he explained, the class would get the promised day off the following Monday. The news was greeted with a deafening roar of approval that lasted until Wriede restored decorum by reminding us that we were not in a *Judenschule* [Jewish school] where lack of discipline was the order of the day. Since none of us had ever attended a *Judenschule*, we were obliged to take the principal's word.

I had followed the morning's proceedings with growing embarrassment, since I was painfully aware that none of the praise heaped on the class by Schürmann and Wriede included me. The only thing that helped somewhat to restore my morale was the thought of not having to return to school until Tuesday. Thus, by the time school let out at noon, I had bounced back and was chatting and laughing with several classmates as we crossed the lobby on our way out. Just before leaving the building, I heard a familiar voice shout, "You, come here!"

When I turned around, I saw the principal standing in the door of his office. I knew at once that he meant me, since he had never addressed me by my name.

"Come in a minute; I have to talk to you," he announced.

Final Insult

Suddenly, a sinking feeling got hold of me. I had no idea of what the principal wanted to discuss with me, but I was convinced that it was nothing I wanted to hear. My instincts proved only too right.

"I am a fair man," Wriede started, "and I hope you are fair, too. Are you?"

I assured him that I was fair, indeed.

"That's good," he continued, "because then you'll agree that it would be very unfair to give you a day off when you have done nothing to earn it. You wouldn't want that, would you—to get something you didn't earn?"

Now the cat was out of the bag and I realized how Wriede had been setting me up.

"Well, would you?" the principal insisted.

"No," I finally replied, "but—"

"That's good," Wriede cut me off, "because I have already spoken with Herr Dutke, and he's told me that it is all right with him if you spend a day in his class. So on Monday morning you report to Herr Dutke. Do you understand?"

"I understand," I answered, although at that time, at age ten, I really hadn't been able to figure out why Wriede treated me so meanly.

"That's all. *Heil Hitler!*" Wriede dismissed me.

"*Heil Hitler!*" I saluted and walked out of his office and home.

I never told my mother what had happened. I was certain that had I done so, she would have defied Wriede by keeping me out of school on Monday, regardless of the consequences to her. So to keep her from getting upset and to avoid trouble, I went to school on Monday as if nothing had happened, as a special "guest" in Herr Dutke's class, where, after being welcomed with a sneer, I had to put up for an entire day with Dutke's snide racist remarks.

The Impact of the Nuremberg Laws

Cynthia Crane

Ursula Bosselman's childhood in Hamburg, Germany, appeared to be an ordinary one—punctuated with advent candles, summer trips, and the singing of "Hitler songs." Her parents were accomplished members of distinguished families. But as the following excerpt illustrates, before World War II, with the enactment of Germany's Nuremberg Laws, shadows began to appear over her family life. At first, the problems were relatively innocuous—she feared her disabled younger sister might blurt out unwise political jokes, and Ursula's education choices were limited. Then a revelation marked the deepening of the shadows, as Ursula learned that, even though her mother had been baptized in the Dutch Reformed Church as a child, she was still considered Jewish and not fully German under the increasingly harsh Nazi rule. By the time the war was over, Ursula's younger sister had been threatened with sterilization, her Jewish grandmother had committed suicide and her mother had been sent to a concentration camp.

Cynthia Crane is an assistant English professor at Raymond Wallace College in Cincinnati, Ohio. Years after the war she wrote a book on women who had suffered under the Nuremberg Laws, including Bosselman. Bosselman survived the war, become a theologian (although she still felt distant from her Jewish background), worked in various countries, and returned to settle in her hometown in the 1990s.

What struck me about Hamburg were the cast-over, deep shadows, years before we had to darken the windows in the evening because of plane attacks. In spite of that, I have come back to this city after exactly forty years, for I have my roots here. I love my father city. It is, yes, really the city of my father. I love the Alster with the white fleet, the many yachts and swans. And

Cynthia Crane, *Divided Lives: The Untold Stories of Jewish-Christian Women in Nazi Germany*. New York: St. Martin's Press, 2000. Copyright © 2000 by Cynthia Crane. Reproduced by permission of Palgrave Macmillan.

the large old houses between Rabenstraße and Eichen Park. And naturally, Jungfernstieg and the Neuen Wall. I love Uhlenhorst, where we lived in the Overbeckstraße, went on Graumannsweg to the school, and were confirmed in St. Gertrud Church. And I add to that Eppendorfer Landstraße where we survived the war and all of the terror, and where my parents' apartment stood until 1985. In addition, around the corner, not far away from Hamburg, are the Baltic Sea and the North Sea. One sensed the sea wind near us and it was suggested that sometimes you could smell it. I have a special love for the ocean. Already as a small child, I had dug on Timmendorfer beach on the Baltic. Keitum in Sylt became our summer paradise. Berlin is the city of my mother and, above all, the city of my grandmother. Because it was always the autumn holiday in our youth that we spent at our grandmother's in Berlin, the street names—Wilmersdorf, Charlottenburg, Lietzenburger and Emser Straße, Kufürstendamm, Unter den Linden, Brandenburger Tor, Grünewald, Potsdam—sounded like children's melodies that accompanied the falling green and yellow leaves. We traveled a last time in peace on Easter to Berlin. That was in 1933. After that the forthcoming events [of Hitler's Reich] crept up on us children like something eerie and unnamable. We were only aware in part, but not in whole, because everybody's parents remained silent as long as possible.

Life in the Family

On Easter 1936 I left the private middle school, Mittell und Redlich, in Hamburg's Graumannsweg with an intermediate secondary school certificate. Even belatedly, I cannot say whether and how this school altered under National Socialism. Did we have "party-friendly" teachers? I believe no. I recall there *was* a "flags parade" on the playground. This "flags parade" was probably obligatory for all schoolchildren. One episode occupied our minds for some days, although we really did not grasp its significance. We sat in a school performance of [Friedrich Schiller's] *William Tell* in the Hamburger *Schauspielhaus* [theater]. It was explained to us beforehand that we, in the manner of *Rütli-Schwur* [a Swiss oath] would have to stand up and raise our arm in a Hitler *Gruß* [salute with outstretched arm]. At the words "We want to be a united people of brothers, no trouble and danger separate us," we stood up solemnly. A girl from my sister's class took a comb out of her pocket, lifted it over her head, and combed her hair. When we reported this at home, my parents exchanged meaningful glances. The recalcitrant girl was kicked out of school. I was fifteen years old.

We were children of our time. On school excursions we sang the Hilter songs. They were easy to sing. We didn't understand the contents at all. What did it mean: "Red front and Reaction?" We were, like everyone else, exposed to propaganda; for example, in the newsreels and films shown at that time. I remember a trip at Pentecost to Dreisacker near Glücksburg [a town near the Danish border in Schleswig-Holstein]. We rode in an open car of Uncle Diederich D. Gisela and I greeted the cars driving past us with the Hitler greeting. We had a lot of fun with that. At the time, we knew nothing about the Nürnberg [Nuremberg] Laws.

My father was a lawyer. He hailed from an old Hamburg family that still adhered to formal traditions. Thus, my mother used the formal *Sie* (you) with her father-in-law, and he with her. This was a Hanseatic tradition. Similarly, my father's father probably stood on a pedestal for *him*. Although my father was a good lawyer, he had not selected his occupation very sensibly. His main interests turned to literature and theater. In those subjects, he was a walking dictionary to us children because he knew about all of the operas' and plays' main figures and he knew which well-known singers and actors had played in what roles in specific years. The director of the Schauspielhaus and the Thalia Theater, among others, befriended him, and he was also the legal advisor of the Thalia Theater for several years. In this funtion he appeared one time as the Thalia Theater's defender in a case. It was said that an employee had lost his life on a fast, down-moving elevator. It is the only time that I heard my father deliver a summary in the courtroom. It made a huge impression on me. My father possessed, as well, considerable general knowledge, and spoke, like my mother, fluent French, for he had completed one part of his studies in Lausanne. . . .

A Loving Family

My parents loved each other despite being different. My father didn't make a mistake in marrying my Jewish mother. In this generation: Once married, not to be discussed. There wasn't a question about it. It was a loving relationship. It was clear that one person would remain faithful to the other. It was deeply rooted for him. Hanseatic that he was. Later my mother had to do everything alone. We couldn't hire anybody. My mother fulfilled this role fantastically well. Never complained. Never said anything. Everything was strange and new and stressful. She had a strong character.

My mother came from a Posener family. I don't think it was difficult that she was Jewish because she was baptized as a child. Her mother and brother were also baptized. Opapa, as we called my grandfather, owned a cannery there that he expanded considerably after the move to Berlin. He had already died in 1923. I was just five years old, yet I can still remember him. I also remember that in my grandparents' bedroom, a big, greenish lion's head hovered over the wash bowl and whenever you pushed a button water flowed out of his mouth.

This grandfather left my maternal grandmother a considerable fortune. According to my mother's statements, her childhood and youth were full of promise and lucky. Many times she spoke proudly about trips that both she and her brother Helmuth took with their parents—trips that many people in those times were not in the position to finance. For a year after finishing school, she stayed and worked in a *Pension* near Paris that she would rave about in her old age. I own her diary written in German script that records this time. Up until her marriage she played violin very well. My parents' marriage took place in summer 1917 in Berlin—my father in "near uniform," my mother a very beautiful young bride. We three sisters, I, Gisela, and Irmi, were born in 1918, 1920, and 1923 respectively. My parent's marriage was—as only I can arrange in my mind in retrospect—severely burdened by the birth of my youngest sister, Irmi, who made it through a so-called birth trauma and was viewed as physically handicapped. My father could not cope with this "insult" that stained his reputation. Only thirty years later was he really reconciled with his daughter. My mother had a very special love for this child and fought for her like a lioness. Later this was necessary. . . .

Irmi was behind developmentally for her age but, in her own fashion, was extremely intelligent. We all grew up together, and you don't notice when you have an ill sister. Irmi wasn't treated as sick but healthy. She was nice and kind, and had a marvelous sense of humor and an incredible head for jokes. No one had negative feelings towards her. During the Hitler years, a great fear sometimes gripped us that she might pass on political jokes to the wrong people. However, she knew instinctively where and when she could tell them. Often I envied Irmi her tanned complexion. In the summer at the ocean she became cocoa brown, and her light hair bleached almost white. Irmi couldn't sit until she was four and couldn't walk until she was six. She had trouble with speaking or with parroting back the teacher's words, but she balanced that out with bouts of humor. In this way she was hard to describe. *Sie hat alles mitbekommen* [she took everything in]. Although she went to the same school as we and even the four prep years [beginning four classes of the six in high school], she had to take each class twice. Job training was not yet available for the handicapped, so she stayed home.

My parents had persuaded us not to do an *Abitur* [pre-college exam]. At first, we did not know the real reason. My parents said taking the *Abitur* served no purpose for a woman. My mother never explicitly told me "You're not allowed to do that because of your Jewish blood," which was really the truth. Gisela participated for a while in the BDM [Nazi youth group] because she insisted on it. We didn't realize that we could not be drafted into "work service" because of our Jewish blood. . . .

Isolated

In October 1936 Gisela and I returned home. One afternoon our mother got us together for "a meeting." In my memory, it was horridly dark in the living room where we were supposed to sit together. My mother disclosed that she was of Jewish background, that is, "not Aryan." My mother was baptized together with her brother at the age of three in January 1898 in the Dutch Reformed Church in Hanau and on March 11, 1910, confirmed in Berlin. My grandmother, Hedwig Moral, was confirmed on February 13, 1903, in Berlin and had declared her resignation from Judaism and her simultaneous conversion to the religious organization of the Protestant church. Grandfather Moral was a dissenter but received his "last rites" at his cremation in 1923.

However, after Hitler's Nuremberg race laws of 1935, the facts of the case didn't count. It didn't matter whether or not you were baptized or confirmed. Because of the race laws, which had not been explained earlier to us, we could not do an *Abitur*, be in the BDM or in the "work service," and could not take up any kind of profession that required a state exit exam. She didn't say that we also were forbidden to marry. My mother told me many years later that I had cried. It was not common to cry in our house. I believe also that I never again shed tears over it. The shock was too great. From one minute to the next everything changed: There was no future, no destination, no joy. Suddenly we were no longer Germans, and according to the official state version we were no longer Christian even though Pastor Speckmann just had confirmed us a year ago. And we hadn't the slightest notion about Jewish culture or religion. Hence, we also didn't belong to that side! Before I knew what was going on, I stood by my mother, but after I knew, I think my relationship with her became more difficult. Perhaps I blamed her for our miserable situation. Of course she was blameless. For young people today it is hard to imagine that at home we asked no questions. It sufficed that indefinability hung in the air. We especially would have never asked about Hitler's Reich. To probe the feelings of others, especially parents, was taboo. The door to the world slammed brutally shut. There I stood at eighteen looking into nothingness.

Yet life continued. After a long search, I found I could take courses in stenography and typing at the business and language school. After that I worked for a year and a half for an acquaintance of my parents in a very small company for agricultural machinery and products. This field was totally uninteresting to me, but at least I earned my first income. At this time I wrote very melancholy poems. A friendly doctor, who visited us one time, said that he had never before seen a young girl at my age that looked as miserable as I.

From the Perspective of the Powerful

CHAPTER 2

Chapter Preface

Historians agree that the First World War (1914–1918) was devastating to the people of Europe and left deep physical and psychological scars. About 21 million soldiers were wounded and 10 million were killed in fighting that used gruesome new weapons such as machine guns, flamethrowers, and poison gas. The young Adolf Hitler, future leader of the Nazi Party, was one of the wounded soldiers.

The economic results of the war were equally severe. Germany, as one of the losers, was severely punished by having to pay crippling reparations and suffering the loss of territories. These humiliations created a great deal of unrest in Germany during the 1920s and 1930s. Many people could not find jobs, and inflation was so rampant that at times the German currency became almost worthless. Both the German legislature and the streets of Germany were scenes of frequent, sometimes violent, strikes and clashes, which further frightened the populace. Many Germans thought that order and prosperity would never return to their country, especially when the Great Depression began in 1929.

The Nazi Party was born during this period of unrest after World War I. Many of its leaders had suffered financial hardships along with the rest of the German people and had difficulty finding jobs. Some of them found jobs through their connections with the Nazi Party. Although some Germans thought the early Nazi Party—the National Socialist German Workers' Party—was laughable or repulsive, to many others the Nazi message offered hope. People warmed to the message expressed by Hitler and other Nazi leaders: Germany was a proud nation that was being persecuted; Germans comprised an elevated race with a great destiny; and economic salvation and order were just around the corner if Germans followed the leadership of the Nazis.

The personality of Hitler aided the acceptance of Nazi ideals by the German people. This can be hard for people from other societies half a century later to understand—in films, they see a short man with a Charlie Chaplin mustache, angrily gesticulating as he shouts in a foreign language. But, although some of Hitler's contemporaries were repulsed by his aura and found him bizarre, many Germans found his personality extremely attractive and reported positive emotional reactions upon meeting him. And Hitler also won the support of large groups of people; his speeches, along with the pomp that frequently accompanied them, elicited near-religious reactions even from initially skeptical audiences.

Undoubtedly, the dire situation that existed in Germany contributed to the emotional reaction many Germans had to leaders promising salvation. Moreover, the Nazis, once they came to power in the early 1930s, delivered on many of their economic promises. As a result, the German economy recovered more quickly from the Great Depression than the economies of many other nations.

But, from the start, Nazi leaders poisoned their message by creating scapegoats on whom they could focus the nation's ire. The rhetoric of Nazi leaders was characterized by a strident anger against their enemies. The German people not only were a noble race, Hitler said, they would be nobler still if they could root out inferior racial elements such as Jews, dark-skinned people, and people who were thought to have genetic diseases.

Another fatal flaw in Nazi leaders' approach was the degree to which it relied on strong-arm tactics rather than democratic processes and the rule of law. Many Nazi policies, such as the Nuremberg Laws, which restricted the rights of Jews and outlawed mixed unions, were put into effect simply via decree. Similarly, instead of the regular courts, special courts that lacked due process were set up to aid the Nazis in their roundups of criminals and opponents. Although some Germans resisted these totalitarian moves, many others remained silent, probably because they were happy that at least Nazi leaders appeared to be restoring order to a dangerously chaotic society.

The fact that this order was being created by leaders who showed ruthless, totalitarian, or even psychotic tendencies from the beginning apparently did not concern many Germans. Whether the German people's lack of concern about their leaders' flaws was due to desperation, the famed propensity in German culture for order, an underlying tendency toward racial/ethnic prejudice in Germans, Hitler's mesmerizing and deceptive personality, or some other factor is still debated. But unfortunately, the brutal results of the thinking and policies of the leaders of Nazi Germany are today overwhelmingly clear.

The Fuehrer's Everyday Life

Albert Speer

Few people had the opportunity to get to know Nazi leader Adolf Hitler as well as Albert Speer, who Hitler considered a friend. Speer was the official architect of the Nazi Party. During World War II, he served as the minister for armaments and as an economic planner. After the war, he was sentenced to twenty years in prison for war crimes. While in prison, he wrote a memoir about his years in the top ranks of the Third Reich. In the following selection, Speer relates his memories of Hitler. He recounts trips to the mountains and private dinners, and he describes Hitler's relationship with Eva Braun, his attitude toward children, even his taste in gifts and flowers—many details that reveal the character of the popular leader.

After two or three days in Munich, Hitler usually ordered preparations for the drive to "the mountain"—Obersalzberg. We rode over dusty highways in several open cars; the autobahn to Salzburg did not exist in those days, although it was being built on a priority basis. Usually the motorcade stopped for coffee in a village inn at Lambach am Chiemsee, which served delicious pastries that Hitler could scarcely ever resist. Then the passengers in the following cars once more swallowed dust for two hours, for the column rode in close file. After Berchtesgaden came the steep mountain road full of potholes, until we arrived at Hitler's small, pleasant wooden house on Obersalzberg. It had a wide overhanging roof and modest interior: a dining room, a small living room, and three bedrooms. The furniture was bogus old-German peasant style and gave the house a comfortable petit-bourgeois look. A brass canary cage, a cactus, and a rubber plant intensified this impression. There were swastikas on knickknacks and pillows embroidered by admiring women, combined with, say, a rising sun or a vow of "eternal loyalty." Hitler com-

---

Albert Speer, *Inside the Third Reich*. New York: The Macmillan Company, 1970. Copyright © 1970 by The Macmillan Company. All rights reserved. Reproduced by permission.

mented to me with some embarrassment: "I know these are not beautiful things, but many of them are presents. I shouldn't like to part with them."

Soon he emerged from his bedroom, having changed out of his jacket into a Bavarian sports coat of light-blue linen, which he wore with a yellow tie. Usually he fell to talking about his building plans.

A few hours later a small Mercedes sedan would drive up with his two secretaries, Fräulein Wolf and Fräulein Schröder. A simple Munich girl would usually be with them. She was pleasant and fresh-faced rather than beautiful and had a modest air. There was nothing about her to suggest that she was a ruler's mistress: Eva Braun.

Keeping Their Distance

This sedan was never allowed to drive in the official motorcade, for no one was to connect it with Hitler. The secretaries also served the function of disguising the mistress's presence. I could only wonder at the way Hitler and Eva Braun avoided anything that might suggest an intimate relationship—only to go upstairs to the bedrooms together late at night. It has always remained incomprehensible to me why this needless, forced practice of keeping their distance was continued even in this inner circle whose members could not help being aware of the truth.

Eva Braun kept her distance from every one of Hitler's intimates. She was the same toward me too; that changed only in the course of years. When we became more familiar with one another I realized that her reserved manner, which impressed many people as haughty, was merely embarrassment; she was well aware of her dubious position in Hitler's court.

During those early years of our acquaintanceship Hitler, Eva Braun, an adjutant, and a servant were the only persons who stayed in the small house; we guests, five or six of us, including [Private Secretary] Martin Bormann and Press Chief Dietrich, as well as the two secretaries, were put up in a nearby pension.

Awesomeness of the Abyss

Hitler's decision to settle on Obersalzberg seemed to point to a love of nature. But I was mistaken about that. He did frequently admire a beautiful view, but as a rule he was more affected by the awesomeness of the abysses than by the harmony of a landscape. It may be that he felt more than he allowed himself to express. I noticed that he took little pleasure in flowers and considered them entirely as decorations. Some time around 1934, when a delegation of Berlin women's organizations was planning to welcome Hitler at Anhalter Station and hand him flowers, the head of the organization called Hanke, then the Propaganda Minister's secretary, to ask what Hitler's favorite flower was. Hanke said to me: "I've telephoned around, asked the adjutants, but there's no answer. He hasn't any." He reflected for a while: "What do you think, Speer? Shouldn't we say edelweiss? I think edelweiss sounds right. First of all it's rare and then it also comes from the Bavarian mountains. Let's simply say edelweiss!" From then on the edelweiss was officially "the Fuehrer's flower." The incident shows how much liberty party propaganda sometimes took in shaping Hitler's image.

Hitler often talked about mountain tours he had undertaken in the past. From a mountain climber's point of view, however, they did not amount to much. He rejected mountain climbing or alpine skiing: "What pleasure can there be in prolonging the horrible winter artificially by staying in the mountains?" His dislike for snow burst out repeatedly, long before the catastrophic winter campaign of 1941–42. "If I had my way I'd forbid these sports, with all the accidents people have doing them. But of course the mountain troops draw their recruits from such fools."

Trailing Along

Between 1934 and 1936 Hitler still took tramps on the public forest paths, accompanied by his guests and three or four plainclothes detectives belonging to his SS bodyguard. At such times Eva Braun was permitted to accompany him, but only trailing along with the two secretaries at the end of the file. It was considered a sign of favor when he called someone up to the front, although conversation with him flowed rather thinly. After perhaps half an hour Hitler would change partners: "Send the press chief to me," and the companion of the moment would be demoted back to the rear. Hitler set a fast pace. Frequently other walkers met us; they would pause at the side of the path, offering reverent greetings. Some would take up their courage, usually women or girls, and address Hitler, whereupon he would respond with a few friendly words. . . .

Eva Braun was allowed to be present during visits from old party associates. She was banished as soon as other dignitaries of the Reich, such as cabinet ministers, appeared at the table. Even when Goering and his wife came, Eva Braun had to stay in her room. Hitler obviously regarded her as socially acceptable only within strict limits. Sometimes I kept her company in her exile, a room next to Hitler's bedroom. She was so intimidated that she did not dare leave the house for a walk. "I might meet the Goerings in the hall."

In general Hitler showed little consideration for her feelings. He would enlarge on his attitude toward women as though she were not present: "A highly intelligent man should take a primitive and stupid woman. Imagine if on top of everything else I had a woman who interfered with my work! In my leisure time I want to have peace. . . . I could never marry. Think of the prob-

Hitler's speeches elicited near-religious reactions from many Germans. Here, he addresses the Hitler Youth.

lems if I had children! In the end they would try to make my son my successor. Besides, the chances are slim for someone like me to have a capable son. That is almost always how it goes in such cases. Consider [renowned German writer] Goethe's son—a completely worthless person! . . . Lots of women are attracted to me because I am unmarried. That was especially useful during our days of struggle. It's the same as with a movie actor; when he marries he loses a certain something for the women who adore him. Then he is no longer their idol as he was before."

Hitler believed that he had a powerful sexual appeal to women. But he was also extremely wary about this; he never knew, he used to say, whether a woman preferred him as the Chancellor or as Adolf Hitler, and as he often remarked ungallantly, he certainly did not want witty and intelligent women about him. In making such remarks he was apparently not aware of how offensive they must have been to the ladies present. On the other hand Hitler could sometimes behave like a good head of a family. Once, when Eva Braun was skiing and came to tea rather late, he looked uneasy, kept glancing nervously at the clock, and was plainly worried that she might have had an accident.

The Facts of Everyday Life

Eva Braun came of a family of modest circumstances. Her father was a schoolteacher. I never met her parents; they never appeared and continued to live as befitted their station until the end. Eva Braun, too, remained simple; she dressed quietly and wore the inexpensive jewelry that Hitler gave her for Christmas or her birthdays: usually semiprecious stones worth a few hundred marks at most and actually insulting in their modesty. Bormann would present a selection, and Hitler would choose these trinkets with what seemed to me petit-bourgeois taste.

Eva Braun had no interest in politics. She scarcely ever attempted to influence Hitler. With a good eye for the facts of everyday life, however, she did sometimes make remarks about minor abuses in conditions in Munich. Bormann did not like that, since in such cases he was instantly called to account. She was sports-loving, a good skier with plenty of endurance with whom my wife and I frequently undertook mountain tours outside the enclosed area. Once Hitler actually gave her a week's vacation—when he himself was not at Obersalzberg, of course. She went to Zürs with us for a few days. There, unrecognized, she danced with great passion into the wee hours of the morning with young army officers. She was very far from being a modern Madame Pompadour; for the historian she is interesting only insofar as she set off some of Hitler's traits.

Out of sympathy for her predicament I soon began to feel a liking for this unhappy woman, who was so deeply attached to Hitler. In addition, we were linked by our common dislike for Bormann, although at that time what we resented most was the coarseness with which he was raping the beauty of nature at Obersalzberg and betraying his wife. When I heard at the Nuremberg Trial that Hitler had married Eva Braun in the last day and a half of his life, I felt glad for her—even though I could sense even in this act the cynicism with which Hitler had treated her and probably women in general.

I have often wondered whether Hitler felt anything like affection for children. He certainly made an effort when he met them, whether they were the children of acquaintances or unknown to him. He even tried to deal with them in a paternally friendly fashion, but never managed to be very convincing about it. He never found the proper easy manner of treating them; after a few benign words he would soon turn to others. On the whole he regarded children as representatives of the next generation and therefore took more pleasure in their appearance (blond, blue-eyed), their stature (strong, healthy), or their intelligence (brisk, aggressive) than in their nature as children. His personality had no effect whatsoever upon my own children.

The Kommandant and His Wife

Gitta Sereny

Hungarian-born author Gitta Sereny has written extensively about German and Nazi society. In this selection, she interviews Franz Stangl, who commanded two Nazi extermination camps in Poland during World War II, and his wife Theresa. The couple fled Europe after the war, but Franz Stangl was arrested in Brazil many years later and tried in Germany in 1970.

Sereny focuses on the factors that shaped the Stangls' actions, their feelings of being trapped by circumstances, and what they could have done to resist the terrible events that took place at Sobibor, one of the camps where Franz Stangl worked. The interview below was conducted in 1971, when Stangl was in prison in Germany awaiting the appeal of his life sentence. Stangl talks about the memorable vacation his family took in 1942 near Sobibor, when Theresa learned that vast numbers of Jews were being systematically murdered in the camp's gas chambers.

"*Did you want your family to come to visit you in Poland?*" I asked [Franz] Stangl.

"I wanted to see them, of course. But don't you see what the fact that they were allowed to come meant? Globocnik [Stangl's supervisor] had said to me, months before, that I needed leave. But they weren't going to let me go home, like other people. I was in danger, it was quite obvious. And they were making damn sure I knew about it."

Stangl's wife and two little girls, six and four, arrived very soon after his wife [Theresa] had written . . . and they all went to stay with the surveyor, Baurath Moser, in Chelm, twenty miles or so from the camp.

"*Were you officially on leave then, or did you have to go to [the extermination camp] Sobibor during that time?*"

"While we were in Colm [Chelm], I was on leave."

Gitta Sereny, *Into That Darkness: From Mercy Killing to Mass Murder*. New York: McGraw-Hill Book Company, 1974. Copyright © 1974 by Gitta Sereny. Reproduced by permission of the publisher.

"Did your wife ask you what you were doing in Sobibor? What sort of camp it was?"

"Very little then: as I told you she was used to my not being able to speak to her of service matters. And we were so glad just to be together. . . . I didn't have any official instructions how long my leave was to be, how long the family would be allowed to stay, or anything. After about three weeks I went to see Höfle [a colleague] and asked him. He said, 'Why make waves? If nobody's said anything to you, why not just keep them here for a while? Find a place to stay nearby, and don't worry'."

"What did you think that meant?"

"I was so glad to have them there, you know; it was such a relief, I just decided not to think, just to enjoy it. I found rooms for us on an estate just a few kilometres from Sobibor camp, near the village. It was a fish-hatchery belonging to Count Chelmicki [he said 'Karminsky', but Frau Stangl corrected this later]."

"How far exactly was that from the camp?"

"Five kilometres."

Pan Gerung, the custodian of Sobibor, remembered the fish-hatchery well thirty years later; it had been demolished a year before I visited Poland. But he and his wife were dubious about the Stangl family having stayed there. "You are probably confusing it with a big white house the Germans built as a kind of country club for their officers, on the other side of the lake. They used to go there for weekends, for the fishing—and other days too, in the evenings. An enormous amount of drinking went on there, and other things. Poles weren't allowed in."

I replied that I was sure it was the fish-hatchery the Stangls had stayed at—no doubt they had requisitioned rooms there because the other place was unsuitable for small children.

"But the fish-hatchery was four kilometres from the camp, through the woods," said Pan Gerung. "If he really rode through these woods, on his own—why, anyone could have shot him, any time." This Polish inhabitant of a different Sobibor, in a different age, sounded honestly puzzled, even amazed. And what he said was true: everyone in those parts knew what Sobibor was; everyone knew Stangl was the camp's Kommandant; anyone—if for no other reason than a gesture—could have shot him on those almost daily rides through the woods. But no one did.

The Truth Slips Out

"The Chelmickis," I said to Stangl, *"must have known or guessed what was going on at Sobibor. However secret an operation it was, there must have been rumours. Did your wife still not know?"*

"The Chelmickis were very nice. But I don't think they would have dared to talk about it even if they had heard rumours." ("... The Jews who worked in the fish-hatchery," Frau Stangl was to write to me later, "were all treated very well. And so was I. ...")

"But my wife *did* find out, though not from them," Stangl said. "One of the non-coms, Unterscharführer Ludwig, came by once while I was out. He had been drinking and he told her about Sobibor. When I got back she was waiting for me. She was terribly upset. She said, 'Ludwig has been here. He told me. My God, what are you doing in that place?' I said, 'Now, child, this is a service matter and you know I can't discuss it. All I can tell you, and you must believe me: whatever is wrong—*I* have nothing to do with it.'"

"Did she believe this, without further questions or arguments?"

He shrugged. "She spoke of it sometimes. But what else could I say to her? It did make me feel, though, that I wanted her away from there. I wanted them to go home. The school term was about to start for the older of the girls anyway. ..." the sentence trailed off.

"It was too difficult having them there now that she knew. Wasn't that it?"

He shrugged his shoulders again and for a moment buried his face in his hands. "Just about then I had a message that I was to come to Warsaw to see Globocnik—by this time he had two offices, one in Warsaw, the other in Lublin. Now it seemed even more urgent to me to get the family home. I got hold of Michel [a colleague] and said that I entrusted my family to him; for him to get them out as quickly as possible. Then I said goodbye to my wife and children and went to Warsaw."

A New Assignment

"When did they leave?"

"Later I found that Michel got them out in four days. But I only found that out after they had gone. And I didn't know what awaited me in Warsaw. I thought that this was probably it—that

I was finally for it. But when I got to Globocnik's office, he was nearly as friendly as he'd been the first time we met. I couldn't understand it. He said, almost as soon as I came in, 'I have a job for you; it is strictly a police assignment.' I knew right away there was something wrong with it, but I didn't know what. He said, 'You are going to Treblinka. We've already sent a hundred thousand Jews up there and nothing has arrived here in money or materials. I want you to find out what's happening to the stuff; where it is disappearing to.'"

"But this time you knew where you were being sent; you knew all about Treblinka and that it was the biggest extermination camp. Here was your chance, here you were, face to face with him at last. Why didn't you say right there and then that you couldn't go on with this work?"

"Don't you see? He had me just where he wanted me; I had no idea where my family was. Had Michel got them out? Or had they perhaps stopped them? Were they holding them as hostages? . . . No, he had me flat: I was a prisoner."

"But even so—even admitting there was danger. Wasn't anything preferable by now to going on with this work in Poland?"

"Yes, that's what we know now, what we can say now. But then?"

"Well, in point of fact, we know now, don't we, that they did not automatically kill men who asked to be relieved from this type of job. You knew this yourself, didn't you, at the time?"

"I knew it *could* happen that they wouldn't shoot someone. But I also knew that more often they *did* shoot them, or send them to concentration camps. How could I know which would apply to me?"

This argument, of course, runs through all of Stangl's story; it is the most essential question at which, over and over, I found myself stopped when talking with him. I didn't know when I spoke with him and I don't know now at which point one human being can make the moral decision for another that he should have the courage to risk death.

However, my reactions to some of the things Stangl said in this part of his account changed slightly subsequently, as a result of my conversations with his wife. These demonstrated very clearly that—if nothing else—he had manipulated events, or his memory of events, to suit his need to rationalize his guilt, his awareness of his guilt or (at that point in our talks) his need to avoid facing it.

Theresa Stangl's Account

"He had written to me soon after he got to Poland saying he was 'constructing'," said Frau Stangl, "but he didn't say what. And all I could think of was how glad I was he wasn't at the front. And then, when he'd been there for a long time without leave [it was interesting that she considered two months 'a long time'], he wrote to say that they were going to let us come to visit him as he was not going to be allowed on leave away from the East at all. And shortly afterwards a Wehrmacht [army] officer arrived with travel papers for us.

"The two children and I travelled out in June. I remember we missed the connection in Cracow; you can imagine what it was like travelling with two small girls in the middle of the war.

"No, I knew nothing—nothing whatever. He met us off the train, and, of course, we hadn't seen him in months, it was just wonderful to see him again. Once again, that was all I could think of. We went to stay in Chelm in the house of the chief surveyor, Baurath Moser. In a way I suppose that was the first time I came into contact with anything to do with Jews [in Poland] because he had two young Jewish girls there, as domestic servants. They were called the two *Zäuseln**—I don't really know why. They were nice girls, helped me with the children and all that. Although I hadn't any notion of the true situation, there were things that made me wonder: you see, the walls of the house were very thin and I would hear Baurath Moser in the room next to ours when I was in bed. He had both the girls—the *Zäuseln*—in there and . . . well . . . he did things to them, you know. It would start every night with his telling them what to take off first and then what next and what to do and so on . . . it . . . it was very embarrassing. And I didn't like what he did to the girls; but, you know, I mainly asked myself, 'Why do they do it? Why don't they just give notice?' That's how little I knew." (Later, in a letter, Frau Stangl mentioned these gifts again—and this time slightly differently: "The two *Zäuseln* in Chelm," she wrote, "were

---

* Probably best translated as "tousle-heads".

always merry, had good food, and were very neat.")

"But I was very glad when Paul [Franz Stangl] told me he had arranged for us to move to the fish-hatchery—it would be better for all of us, and I was glad to get the children away from that house. No, while we were in Chelm, Paul was on leave; it was when we moved to the fish-hatchery that he had to go back to work.

"And one day while he was at work—I still thought constructing, or working at an army supply base—Ludwig came with several other men, to buy fish or something. They brought schnapps, and sat in the garden drinking. Ludwig came up to me—I was in the garden too, with the children—and started to tell me about his wife and kids; he went on and on. I was pretty fed up, especially as he stank of alcohol and became more and more maudlin. But I thought, here he is, so lonely—I must at least listen. And then he suddenly said, '*Fürchterlich*—dreadful, it is just dreadful, you have no idea how dreadful it is.' I asked him 'What is dreadful?'—'Don't you know?' he asked. 'Don't you know what is being done out there?'—'No,' I said, 'What?'—'The Jews,' he answered. 'The Jews are being done away with.'—'Done away with?' I asked. 'How? What do you mean?'—'With gas,' he said. 'Fantastic numbers of them [*Unheimliche Mengen*].'

"He went on about how awful it was and then he said, in that same maudlin way he had, 'But we are doing it for our Führer. For him we sacrifice ourselves to do this—we obey his orders.' And then he said, too, 'Can you imagine what would happen if the Jews ever got hold of *us?*'

"Then I told him to go away. I could hardly think. I was already crying. I took the children into the house. I sat there, staring, staring into an abyss—that's what I saw; *my* husband, my man, my good man, how could he be in this? Was it possible that he actually saw these things being done? . . . My thoughts were in a whirl; what I needed above all was to confront him, to talk to him, to see what he had to say, how he could explain. . . ."

"I Know What You Are Doing"

She left the children playing in their room and went out along the path in the forest she knew he would have to take to ride home. "I walked for a long time and sat down on a tree-trunk to wait for him. When he rode up and saw me from afar, his face lit up—I could see it. It always did—his face always showed his joy the moment he saw me. He jumped off his horse and stepped over—I suppose to put his arm around me. But then he saw at once how distraught I was. 'What's happened?' he asked. 'The children?'

"I said, 'I know what you are doing in Sobibor. My God, how can they? What are *you* doing in this? What is your part in it?' First he asked me how I'd found out, but I just cried and cried; and then he said, 'Look, little one, please calm down, please. You must believe me, I have nothing to do with any of this.' I said, 'How can you *be* there and have nothing to do with it?' And he answered, 'My work is purely administrative and I am there to build—to supervise construction, that's all.'—'You mean you don't see it happen?' I asked. 'Oh yes,' he answered. 'I see it. But I don't *do* anything to anybody.'

"Of course, I didn't know he was the Kommandant: I never knew that. He told me he was the *Höchste Charge*. I asked him what that meant and he said again he was in charge of construction and that he enjoyed the work. I thought, 'My God.'

"I Wanted to Be Convinced"

"We walked back to the house, me crying and arguing and begging him over and over to tell me how he could be in such a place, how he could have allowed himself to get into such a situation. I am sure I made no sense—I hardly knew any more what I was saying. All he did, over and over, was reassure me—or try. That night, I couldn't bear him to touch me. . . . He seemed to understand. He just kept stroking me softly and trying to quiet me. Even so, it was several days before I . . . let him again. And that was only just before he was called to Lublin to see Globocnik. I finally allowed myself to be convinced that his role in this camp was purely administrative—of course I *wanted* to be convinced, didn't I? But anyway—I can't quite remember the sequence of events, but I know I wouldn't have parted from him in anger.

"We were rowing on the lake with the children that day when Michel arrived on the shore. This was the only time I saw him. No, *he* never did anything for us after Paul left. I don't know what Paul meant when he told you it was Michel who 'got us out'. Michel called to us across the lake and said that a message had come through to say that Paul was to report to Globocnik. We rowed back to the shore and Michel said, 'They mean now, at once; you have to come with me right away.'

"We went back to the house and I remember, I helped him get changed and then he left.

Others React

"After he had gone that day I got terribly depressed: you see, although I had allowed him to convince me that he wasn't really part of what was happening, I couldn't forget it; how could I have? That night Countess Chelmicki found me crying. In my terrible need to talk to somebody I told her what I had found out.

"'Don't you think we know?' she asked. 'We've known about it since the beginning. But you must calm yourself; it is dreadful, but there is nothing to be done. We are convinced that your husband is a decent man.' She really cared. She spoke to me—you know—like a friend, intimately and warmly. I was very comforted by her kindness.

"The next day Paul came back, just for a day, or even less. He said he was being transferred, to Treblinka—a place, he said, that was in a terrible mess, where the worst *Schweinereien* were being done, and where it was necessary to make a clean sweep with an iron broom. I said, 'My God, I hope not another place like this one here,' and he said no, he didn't think so—for me not to worry. I said I wanted to go home."

I asked Frau Stangl whether it had not been her husband who told *her* he wanted them to go home.

"No, I told *him*. And, well . . . then he left. I'd told him I wanted to leave as quickly as possible—I didn't want to impose on the Chelmickis a moment longer than necessary. Anyway, the next day Reichleitner came to the fish-hatchery."

Franz Reichleitner, who had been with Stangl at Hartheim, took over as Kommandant of Sobibor after Stangl left. "He said he wanted to have a look around the fish-hatchery," Frau Stangl continued. "Well, of course I knew him, you know, because he had married my friend Anna Baumgartner from Steyr and so I felt I had something in common with him; I trusted him you know, so I said, 'You know, if I thought that my Paul had anything to do with the awful things which are being done at Sobibor, I wouldn't stay with him another day.'

"He answered quite spontaneously, you know, not thinking it over at all. He said right away, 'My God, Frau Stangl,' he said, 'but your husband has absolutely *nothing* to do with that. . . . Your husband's part in this is purely administrative.'" (Before Frau Stangl told me this, she had already testified at the trial, that after the war, in Brazil, Gustav Wagner had also told her that her husband had had nothing to do with the extermination of the Jews in Sobibor.) "Well," she went on, "to be truthful, that really did relieve my mind and lighten my spirits. After all, unless Paul and Reichleitner had carefully planned it together—and to tell the truth, the possibility did occur to me—the fact that they told me exactly the same thing, in the same words, had to mean it was true. Why otherwise should Reichleitner have bothered to tell me?"

It didn't occur to Frau Stangl then or now that Reichleitner, who had just taken the job over from Stangl, could have found this conversation with his friend's wife awkward on his own account, and might conceivably have been indirectly stating, or justifying, his own case.

"I left a very few days after that," she said. "I think it was Reichleitner who brought me the travel documents signed by Globocnik—it may have been just two or three days after Paul left. I think Reichleitner also drove us to the train in Chelm. And so I went home. I had a letter from Paul soon after, but it said nothing about Treblinka; he had told me I must *never* mention Treblinka nor anything about it, or make any of my 'remarks' in my letters—he knew me so well—as all letters were censored. . . . I didn't see him after that for months. . . ."

"Resl [Theresa Stangl] and the two girls came to stay with me overnight on their way back from Poland," said Helene Eidenböck [Franz Stangl's sister-in-law] in Vienna. "I went to meet them at the East Station. No, she didn't seem very depressed, not that I remember. She said they'd been staying at a fish-hatchery and I saw all their photographs . . . was it then or later, I am not sure—of him too, yes, in that white jacket, with the children, and a big dog too I remember. . . . Later, of course, when we read what he was—I thought of that photo and thought, 'It only needed the riding crop and there he was, just as they described him at the trial. . . .'"

Children of the Reich

Gitta Sereny

Forty-five years after the end of the Nazi Third Reich, an Israeli psychologist interviewed forty-nine German men and women who were the offspring of high-ranking Nazis close to Hitler. Later, some of these "children" met regularly in a support group. They had been unable to share their knowledge with almost anyone because the topic of the relationship between Hitler's aides and their children had been taboo in postwar Germany. The meetings prompted relief, some resentment and the airing of long-buried memories. In this selection, author Gitta Sereny, well-known for writing about her experiences in Europe under the Nazis, explains her interviews with members of the support group.

The setting is the quiet, comfortable living room of a house in a small town nestled in the gentle hills of the Ruhr; the occasion, a seemingly innocuous gathering of middle-aged men and women, grouped around a table laden with coffee and cookies. Yet the Germans here today have come to relive a nightmare, to dredge up events that occurred forty-five years ago, during the Second World War. Some bear household names, and the stories they tell, the pain they convey, seem almost irreconcilable with their apparent 'ordinariness'.

They are, one might say, Hitler's children—the sons and daughters of those who accomplished his terrible work. For half a century they have been unable to talk to anyone about their feelings, their knowledge, their relationships with their parents. And as one listens to them, as one sees their loneliness, a single thought keeps recurring: How many more like them are there?

Gunild, now fifty-seven, hasn't slept without sedatives for decades. She is small, round, charming, with a smile that seems permanently painted on her face. In 1924, one of Gunild's brothers died; he was three months old and had a club-foot. She

---

Gitta Sereny, *The Healing Wound: Experiences and Reflections on Germany, 1938–2001.* New York: W.W. Norton and Company, 2001. Copyright © 2000 by Gitta Sereny. All rights reserved. Reproduced by permission of the publisher.

thinks—though she can barely bring herself to say it—that her father (a doctor, now dead), who served a prison sentence for having been in charge of the euthanasia programme in the Rhineland and for 'clearing' the Cologne area of Jews, had his handicapped son killed.

Others in her family—siblings, cousins and one of her own children—have since died. Only her twenty-four-year-old daughter is left. 'Is God exacting payment from us?' Gunild asks, and trembles for her daughter's life.

Dirk turned fifty this year. His father—head of the Gestapo in Braunschweig, where thousands of forced labourers died at the Göring plant—was hanged in 1948. Twenty years later, Dirk married Lena, a Russian girl from Israel. 'Children?' he says. 'No, we have no children. How could we?' And Lena cries. 'I would have liked a child,' she says. . . .

Waiting for Father

Forty-nine-year-old 'Monika' (an assumed name) was an illegitimate child and never met her father, though he has dominated her thoughts for years. She spent the first three years of her life in a Children's Home of the *Lebensborn*, the organization set up by the SS to encourage the breeding of 'perfect' Aryan children. Monika remembers the nurses there as kind, even tender. Life after the war was more difficult. She lived with her mother, a lonely, secretive woman, who claimed Monika's wonderful father was missing in action. Monika believed that her father, like so many others, was a POW of the Soviets and that he, like other fathers, would eventually come home. In the meantime, she tried to make her mother love her. '*Now* you are happy to have a girl, aren't you?' she asked after a spectacular scholastic success at the age of eight. 'No,' her mother answered, 'I am not.' In this cold environment, all of Monika's childish dreams and longings were focused on the loving and warm father her mother constantly cried for. Every time someone came to the door, she would run to watch her mother open it, hoping to catch her parents' first words to each other; every time her mother baked a cake, Monika would put a bit of hers aside for him.

In fact, she would later learn, by that time her father was already dead—executed for war crimes. He had been an early member of the SS and an organizer of the first nationwide pogrom, the *Kristallnacht* ('Night of Broken Glass'), in November 1938, when carefully synchronized violence against Jewish people and their property erupted in major German cities. As the commanding SS general of the *Einsatzgruppen* (the Special Action Groups) in the Soviet Union and the Baltics in 1941, he had been in charge of the murder of half a million or more Jews and tens of thousands of non-Jewish Russians. He was hanged in Riga in February 1946.

'I only discovered the details about eight years ago,' says his daughter, 'and I think it's true that as of then I always wanted to punish, hurt myself; if I had this father, I told myself . . . I must pay for it.'

Memories of a 'Tender' Uncle

Thomas Heydrich, very young-looking at fifty-nine, is a well-known actor who reads and sings all over Germany, mostly from works by Jewish poets. He has many memories of his uncle, Reinhard Heydrich, who was also his godfather, but never knew him as head of the Gestapo, creator of the 'Final Solution', and 'Protector of Bohemia-Moravia', where he was assassinated on 6 June 1942.

Thomas was eleven years old at the time. For him, Reinhard Heydrich was his father's much-loved older brother, with whom his parents had regularly played bridge; he was also a fine musician, and on Thomas's birthday and for Christmas he would send his chauffeur with extravagant presents.

'I was angry when he was killed,' says Thomas, 'because I was, of course, at that time a "fire and flame" *Pimpf*' [member of a Nazi youth group]. He stops and shakes his head. 'Well,' he continues, 'he was a kind of hero to us; we didn't know anything about politics: we only knew that he was a fantastic sportsman—fencing champion, I think . . . and, of course, always in the papers, standing next to the Führer, our idol. Well, you know . . . And I was sad when he was assassinated because I knew my father would be very sad. My uncle was a very good, tender father,' he says thoughtfully. 'It's almost a cliché now, isn't it, about these appalling men? But that doesn't make it any less true—one just doesn't like to think of it. Can you imagine? Tender?' He repeats the word bitterly.

Hitler's Favorite Godson

Martin Bormann, now sixty, was Hitler's favourite godson. Like Thomas, Martin was a passionate Nazi child, immensely proud of his important father, who was Hitler's personal assistant. (The author Hugh Trevor-Roper has described the elder Martin Bormann as 'the most powerful, the least public, and the most mysterious of all the Nazi leaders . . . In Hitler's last years . . . Bormann reigned undisputed over the court . . . he built around the Führer "a Chinese wall" impenetrable except by his favour.')

Bormann co-signed Hitler's last will and took part in the bizarre burning of the bodies after the double suicide of Hitler and his wife of one day, Eva Braun, during the afternoon of 30 April 1945. He then escaped from the bunker two nights later with the remaining members of Hitler's circle. For twenty-eight years afterward, the secret services of the Western powers were inundated with reports of sightings of Martin Bormann: in South America, in Switzerland, in Spain. In 1973 the Frankfurt police issued a statement that a skeleton discovered in Berlin was Bormann's. 'But I have never been sure of that,' says his oldest son. 'Their proof was unconvincing.'

For fifteen-year-old Martin, the shock of 'the end' was enormous. The night he learned that Hitler had died, eight people in the group with which he was hiding—high officials of the party chancery—committed suicide. 'I, too, was close to killing myself,' he says. 'But I do think that, as time went on, the children of people who had not been at the very top had a much more difficult time than we had: they were left surrounded by silence and lies. In our world, lies were impossible after the war—we knew where our fathers had stood. All we had to do was watch and read and listen, and accept the truth.'

Learning the Truth

Martin Bormann learned the truth while living under a false name with devoutly Catholic Austrian peasants. 'I learned from them what is a good man,' he says. In 1947 he was received into the Catholic Church. For years afterwards, he lived in fear: his father hated Jews—but he hated Catholicism even more. Convinced that he was still alive and in hiding, 'I was afraid he would have me liquidated because I had become a Catholic.'

It took an outsider of sorts to bring together Hitler's children—all of them, I'm bound to say, exceptional people—and encourage them to take issue with the past. Six years ago, a forty-six-year-old Israeli psychologist, Dan Bar-On, on a visiting professorship at the West German University of Wuppertal, realized that not only had the relationships between Hitler's aides and their children never been thoroughly researched, but four decades after the end of the 'thousand-year' Reich the subject was still taboo in Germany.

In 1985, Bar-On had ads inserted in the local papers asking for 'persons whose parents were in the SS or took an active part in . . . persecution and extermination' to contact him. A surprising number of people replied. Bar-On, the Israeli-born son of assimilated German Jews who fled Hamburg in 1933, spent the next two years interviewing forty-nine children of perpetrators in Germany. His book, *Legacy of Silence*, tells (anonymously in all but one case) the stories of thirteen children.

Burden of Guilt

They, who had never spoken to anyone of their terrible legacy, except perhaps to their life partners, agreed to talk to Bar-On, they told me, primarily for two reasons: he was not only an Israeli and a descendant of their fathers' victims, as they were the descendants of the victimizers, but also an academic, a scientist belonging to a 'caring' discipline, who, by 'caring' about them and their feelings, might ease the terrible weight of transferred guilt they carried.

Bar-On's original interest was complicated by a built-in resistance to all things German and although he knew it to be irrational, especially to the children of the Germans who had killed or been instrumental in the murder of his people. The most moving aspect of his undertaking, I found, was the change that gradually took place in him. The pain and the manifest honesty of those he interviewed slowly allowed Bar-On to drop some of his own reserve and lower the barriers of his prejudices. Slowly he came to see them as individuals in dire need, rather than as Germans tainted by their parentage—so much so that his real triumph was perhaps not the publication of the book itself but a conference a year earlier in Wuppertal, which many of the 'children' attended in a show of mutual support. It was there that Bar-On initiated the notion of a self-help group, which would continue the healing process.

Nine 'children' joined this group—the first and only such undertaking in Germany to date. Eight of these, several now under their real names, agreed to be interviewed for this article, a decision they courageously made so that others in the same position might feel able to 'come out' of the isolation their parents had imposed on them.

Looking with Different Eyes

The guiding German spirit behind the group is Konrad Brendler, a professor of education at the University of Wuppertal and a good friend of Bar-On. His own, Catholic parents—bakers by profession—were not Nazis. 'But I, too, a few years ago, found myself looking into their past with different eyes: not, you see, for what they did, but for what—despite their religious commitment—they did *not* do.'

Brendler's family lived in Breslau when he was a child. He recently provoked a confrontation by asking his parents what they remembered about the *Kristallnacht*. 'My father said that the shop next door had been plundered that night and that the owners disappeared—he assumed they had emigrated. He had bought their piano for 300 marks. He added that he had told the movers to drive around the block and bring it from the opposite side so that people wouldn't know he'd bought it from Jews. I asked him whether he knew what happened to Jews when they were removed.

'"Well, they just left," he said, implying it was all voluntary. And my mother—who had been in the habit of slipping unauthorized bread and rolls to Jews she knew—said, "No, don't you remember that transport of Jews we saw in the Klosterstrasse, and on it were our two young doctors—the ones who looked after the children? They weren't on it by choice." And she started to cry. And my father made the sort of disparaging gesture I remember well from my childhood, when he regularly mocked and beat me for the sin of sensitivity. '"Nonsense," he said to my mother, just as he had always said to me. "You are quite wrong. Those doctors weren't among those people at all—they had long been gone." You see, even now, he couldn't face the truth. He had to look away now just as he had looked away then.

A Mania for Respectability

'I have come to ask myself whether the guilt of our parents' generation isn't finally much more encompassing than we thought, with those who "merely" did nothing only fractionally less guilty than those who were actively involved. But, facing that, I also have to look at myself: if my father was basically a coward, and, in his attitude towards me, his least assertive son, a bully, what am I? What—I say it deliberately, as a German—are my potentials under pressure?'

To Brendler, the taboo that parents of the Hitler generation have imposed on their children—whether actively or passively—is not due to shame or feelings of guilt. 'More than anything else, our actions and reactions in Germany—then as now—are due to our mania for *Anständigkeit* (respectability, propriety). It both dictates and exalts conduct at the price of conscience.'

He cites as the most glaring and appalling demonstration of this inverted sense of values [Nazi paramilitary chief Heinrich] Himmler's speech to SS leaders and gauleiters on 4 and 6 October 1943 in Posen, in which he explained in detail the reasons and methods behind the extermination of the Jews. Himmler said he had not considered it justified to exterminate men while permitting their potential avengers—women and children—to live. Logic dictated that the women and children be eliminated, too. 'I think I can say that this—the most difficult order we have been issued so far—was executed without allowing our men . . . to suffer any damage in mind or in spirit,' Himmler told his audience. 'The danger was very real: the line between the two potentials—to become cruel and heartless and to lose respect for human life, or else to turn soft and break down—is incredibly fine . . . To have persisted and at the same time . . . to have remained decent men . . . this is a page of glory in our history which has never been written and is never to be written . . . We must take this secret with us to the grave.

'May I invite you to join us for refreshments next door,' Bormann said when Himmler had finished.

'What I cannot understand,' says Bormann's son, talking about the far-right elements now surfacing in East Germany, 'is how anyone can still defend National Socialism, when—quite aside from living witnesses—the records of these speeches exist in the archives.'

Martin Bormann is tall and thin, with close-cropped grey hair and an ascetic face which belies the humour and warmth that become quickly apparent when he is with people he trusts. The group, I found, treats him gingerly. Although most are children of high-level Nazis, the son of Hitler's closest assistant—who in addition carries his father's name—stands out. Why didn't he ever change his name? 'For two years after the war,' he replies, 'I lived under another name, Martin Bergmann. But as I learned to understand what had happened and became my own person, I decided my name was part of me, as my father and the past were part of me, and I had to live with it.

'My father was very strict,' he continues, 'and strictest with me, because I was the oldest.' In 1940, when Martin was ten, his father heard of a notation in his son's report card from the Berchtesgaden school he attended: 'Lazy; could do better.' Bormann ordered that the boy be sent at once to Feldafing, an élite military-type boarding school of which he himself was chairman. 'Well, that was difficult,' Martin says. 'You see, all the others had been selected specifically for their academic qualifications or else for excellence in sports; I was just *put* there.' Would he say, looking back, that the school brainwashed the students? He smiles. 'They didn't have to brainwash us—there was no boy there who wasn't pre-conditioned. It was quite as strict as my father wanted for me. I never resented it. Well, almost never.'

A Special Audience

There was one occasion, he says, when he did feel bitter. He was thirteen, and, as had become the custom for him as Hitler's godson, when he came home on leave he was summoned to a special audience. Wearing his Feldafing uniform he stood at attention and raised his arm in the formal salute. 'But I made a mistake,' he says. 'Instead of the prescribed "Heil, mein Führer," I said, "Heil Hitler, mein Führer," and before I knew it, my father slapped my face so hard I thought my jaw had cracked, and tears came to my eyes—that too was taboo. I was mortified. Why did he have to do that, right in front of the *Chef?'*

His father periodically inspected the school. 'I was proud of him,' Martin remembers. At one point, when there seemed to be irregularities in the school provision accounts, his father ordered him 'to watch certain members of the kitchen staff. No, I didn't think he was using me as a spy, only that he trusted me enough to confer a difficult job on me.'

From 1941, when Martin was eleven, until the war's end, he spent summers working on the land, and saw his father only rarely. 'It was then very special,' he says. 'Once in 1943, on an estate in the Rhineland, I was allowed to go riding with him. I had a Russian pony, which, of course, couldn't keep up with his big horse, but he'd wait for me. It was a wonderful summer.'

The field hands he worked with there were Polish POWs. 'There were no guards, no problems; they ate with the German staff.'

If the Polish POWs at the farm fared well, were he and his school friends aware that this was not the norm? 'Well, yes,' he says. 'Our school, you see, was quite near Dachau, and there was a prisoner detachment that worked in construction just next to our school. And they were really ill-treated by their Kapos [Jews who acted as police for the Nazis in death camps]. But that meant that we hated the Kapos, who were prisoners too, you see, not the SS.'

'The Stillness of that Moment'

On 23 April 1945, with the Allied forces advancing, Feldafing school was abruptly closed; the other boys were given 100 marks each and told to find their own way home. Martin was taken to join some of his father's staff at a village inn near Salzburg. 'It was very small,' he remembers of the inn's saloon, where the group had gathered. 'We were tightly packed together. It's impossible now to convey the atmosphere. The worst moment was when, at two o'clock in the morning of 1 May, the news of Hitler's death came through. I remember it precisely . . . but I can't describe the stillness of that moment, which lasted . . . for hours. Nobody said anything, but people started to go outside, first one . . . then there was a shot . . . then another, and yet another . . . Not a word inside, no other sound except those shots from outside, but one felt that all of us would have to die.'

And so finally Martin, too, took the gun he had been given

and stepped outside. 'My world was shattered; I couldn't see any future at all. But there was another boy out there—he was 18—a good bit older than I. We sat down on some logs. The air smelled good, the birds sang, and we talked ourselves out of it. If we hadn't had each other at that moment, both of us would have gone—I know it.'

After the War

Unsure what to do, he fell in with a column of the Führer-Leibstandarte, Hitler's personal guard regiment. On 8 May, as they were debating forming 'Werewolf' groups to fight as partisans in the mountains, he and some others came down with food poisoning. 'It was destiny, I think, that made me collapse outside a mountain farm,' he says. 'The peasants had no idea who I was, but they took me in as if I were their own son.'

Every day that summer, the farmers sent him up to the *Alm*—the mountain pasture—with the cattle. 'It was quiet and beautiful; I was alone and could think, and later also read books I borrowed from the nearest library. In the evening, when I came down, the peasant gave me his paper to read. It was a liberal paper, the *Salzburger Nachrichten*, which factually and unemotionally—the only way I could bear to read about it—told the truth about what the Nazis had done.'

'How Good Men Live'

A year later, Martin found a small announcement of his mother's death. 'By that time a great deal had happened, not so much *to* but *in* me. I had seen how good men live, how good men *are*. Querleitner, the peasant, was what I wanted to become: a real Christian.'

In January 1947 a priest accepted him for instruction, and on 4 May, his real name now revealed to the peasant who became his godfather, Martin Bormann was received into the church. What had Querleitner said when the boy told him he was Bormann's son? 'He said, in his broad Austrian accent, that being my godfather was the only thing he shared with Hitler.' After that a priest found his eight brothers and sisters for him; they had been taken in by different families in the South Tyrol. 'At Easter 1950 I was able to go and see them for the first time.'

In September 1947 he had been accepted by the Trappists to begin his religious training, and in 1951 he joined the order of the Heart of Jesus. Until 1971 Martin Bormann was a priest, much of the time as a missionary in Africa. Then, having decided that he was no longer suited to the essential narrowness of religious life, and also having seriously injured his legs in a car accident which threatened to leave him entirely dependent on his order, he was granted a dispensation to leave the priesthood. A year later he was given permission to continue to teach religion and Germanics. By that time, he had been working for several years with a missionary nun who had had similar doubts about her vocation and, prior to his decision and independent of it, had asked her order to release her from her vows.

It had been Cordula who had nursed him back to health. They have now been married for nineteen years and live a quiet and modest life in a small modern flat overlooking a hilly village in the Ruhr. It is filled with hundreds of minutely organized books, many of them theological works, and reference materials. Contrary to a first impression of reserve, they turn out on closer acquaintance to be gentle people, openly tender with each other and concerned about the world.

A Hidden Story

Martin Bormann has not always been sure of his commitment to the therapy group, however. During one meeting, he announces that, after a year and a half of attending, he might drop out—he didn't feel he had much more to contribute.

'You always speak of contributing *to* the group,' Lena tells him. 'Has the group not given you anything?'

Martin doesn't respond to this challenge, and the talk continues around for a while, almost as if he weren't there. And then, as sometimes happens when people sit together for a long time, there is a sudden silence and, just as suddenly, Martin's quiet, grave voice speaks into this silence. He begins to tell a story he has never told to anyone before, a story he has evidently hidden even from himself in that part of the mind where human beings store intolerable memories.

It happened, he says, late in the war, when he was at home on the Berghof (in Berchtesgaden) during a school holiday.

Himmler's secretary and mistress, Frau Pothast, who had borne him two children, then about two and three years old, invited Martin's mother to bring him and his thirteen-year-old sister, Eike, over for tea.

The old farmhouse where Himmler had installed her only a few months before was about a twenty-minute drive in one of the special large black Mercedeses at the disposal of Hitler's top echelon and their families. 'Our chauffeur waited outside and we walked in through a nice wild sort of garden,' Martin says as the memory takes shape. 'And she gave us hot chocolate and cakes. It was nice.' Later, Frau Pothast said she would show them something interesting, a special collection Himmler kept in the house. She led the way up to the attic.

'I Knew It Was All True'

'When she opened the door and we flocked in, we didn't understand at first what the objects in that room were—until she explained, quite scientifically, you know. Tables, and chairs, made of parts of human bodies. There was a chair . . . ' Martin's voice becomes toneless as he describes it; the people around the table have frozen into stillness, and I feel my body go prickly. 'The seat was a human pelvis, the legs human legs—on human feet. And then she picked up one of a stack of copies of *Mein Kampf*—all I could think of was that my father had told me not to bother to read it, as it had been outdated by events. She showed us the cover, made of human skin, and explained that the Dachau prisoners who produced it used the *Rückenhaut*—the skin of the back—to make it.'

The children fled, he says, his mother pushing them ahead of her down the stairs. 'Eike was terribly upset, and I was, too,' he tells us. 'About a year later, when I saw photographs of the horrors of the camps, and people said they must be faked, having seen this, I knew it was all true: I had no doubts at all, ever . . . ' His face is red with stress.

'The swine,' says Dirk.

'To call those people swine,' says Martin Bormann's son, 'is an insult to swine.'

'I loved my father,' he tells me weeks later when we come back to this story late one spring evening at his home. 'I certainly didn't identify this horror with him.' Yet he realizes that for years he entirely suppressed one of the most traumatic experiences of his life. 'I just buried it. It proves the usefulness of the group, doesn't it?' (Eventually he will decide to remain a member.) Does he think Hitler ordered these atrocities performed? 'All big decisions were made only by him, but I doubt that he would have initiated anything like this. Why should he?' Martin says. 'He had others for that. He hated details. He was a great vacillator—I heard my father say this to someone when he didn't know I was around.'

What weighs most heavily on him, he says, is that it was mainly his father who built the protective wall around Hitler that in the final months kept the reality of the war at bay. 'The war was never mentioned at home—perhaps it was his way of protecting us. But I remember one occasion, late in the war, when he told us about a train trip with Hitler. For the first time, Hitler—and my father too—saw the terrible consequences of the bombings. My father was not only appalled himself, but really shaken by Hitler's despair. He said he was convinced that Hitler had to be totally insulated from knowledge about these events if he was to continue to function. Perhaps,' says Martin sadly, 'if he hadn't so insulated him, it would have been stopped sooner.'

The Hitler Youth

Alfons Heck

At the age of seventeen, Alfons Heck commanded three thousand men and boys of the Hitler Youth, which fought suicidally against invading armies at the close of World War II. After many years of soul searching, he came to understand the cruelty of the Nazi regime and decided to speak up about his role in it and what lay behind the participation of children in national political and military matters.

After the war, Heck became a U.S. citizen, published books about his experiences, and undertook speaking engagements with a Jewish survivor of a Nazi death camp. This selection begins with Heck's introduction to politics while listening to a Hitler speech on the radio at his grandfather's farm in Germany, a few miles from its border with France.

I consciously heard the voice of Adolf Hitler and the stirring sounds of the Third Reich he was proclaiming when I was less than five years old. My paternal grandfather Jakob Heck, on whose farm I was raised, had mounted an expensive *Blaupunkt* radio on a teak shelf above his favorite chair in the large kitchen. I usually fell asleep there on his lap after the late national news at 10 o'clock. It was the chaotic year of 1932, when the Communists and Nazis battled each other on the streets of Germany with increasing violence, occasionally drawing the Social Democrats into the fray.

"Mark my words, boy," cried my grandfather, fire in his dark French eyes and waving his ever-present pipe, "these damn fool Communists and Social Democrats hate each other so much that they're going to hand the country over to this crazy Austrian." My grandfather, a devout Catholic, had always voted for the Catholic *Zentrum* Party, but that changed after Hitler was appointed Chancellor on January 30, 1933. On that Monday evening, our kitchen was crowded with family and neighbors. Only a few had radios at home, and none had one as powerful

---

Alfons Heck, *The Burden of Hitler's Legacy*. Frederick, CO: Renaissance House Publishers, 1988. Copyright © 1988 by Alfons Heck. All rights reserved. Reproduced by permission of the publisher.

as ours. It easily brought in not only Berlin, but most European cities. Years later, listening to the BBC from London became an irresistible and dangerous attraction to my Aunt Maria, who lived in fear that I would catch and report her to the *Gestapo* for spreading enemy propaganda.

Among our neighbors, two already stood nearly at attention when Hitler's raspy, but strangely compelling voice filled the room on that night of undisguised triumph. Few Germans can resist marching music, especially when it is interspersed with the promise of national renaissance and punctuated by the singing of torch-bearing columns. Quite in contrast to their usually dour and pessimistic nature, the hard-bitten faces of these farmers showed a sudden glow.

"Do you really think he can pull it off?" asked *Herr* Kaspar, who was close to losing his three cows and meager vineyard in this period of grave depression. Currently more than six million people were out of work, 25 percent of the labor force.

"Nonsense," yelled my grandfather, filling everybody's glass with *Viez*, the apple wine of my hometown that can be as astringent as vinegar. "He isn't going to perform any miracles. It's mostly show, but it's better than having the damn Communists take over."

National Pride Restored

Less than two years later, my grandfather and nearly all our neighbors were solidly behind Hitler, and not only because of his astonishing success in creating employment. Equally important, he had restored his people's pride as Rhineland Germans who had been under French occupation since the infamous 1919 Treaty of Versailles. The terms of that document had plunged the country into more than a decade of political turmoil. France, and to a lesser degree the unprotesting British, handed Hitler the first and perhaps most decisive of his bloodless victories, by allowing fewer than 3,000 German troops to re-enter the region, unchallenged by the vastly superior French Army, which sat placidly on its vaunted Maginot Line. That was on March 7, 1936, and the 8,000 people of Wittlich went wild with joy when they saw our troops. That evening, perched on the shoulders of my Uncle Franz, surrounded by what seemed to be all of the population, I briefly glimpsed Adolf Hitler, but more impressive was the unrestrained rapture he evoked in the delirious crowd. For the first time I understood what *Herr* Becker, our elementary school teacher, meant when he said we were now *ein Reich, ein Volk, ein Führer*, one nation, one country, one leader.

All children are defenseless receptacles, waiting to be filled with wisdom or venom by their parents and educators. We who were born into Nazism never had a chance unless our parents were brave enough to resist the tide and transmit their opposition to their children. There were few of those. The majority of Germans lined up solidly behind Hitler, once he had proven he could indeed wreak fundamental changes.

A Separate Path

I might have been one of the few, had I been raised by my parents. My father, the oldest son, would have been first heir to the farm, had he been extremely patient. . . .

When my father was given the choice of waiting for the farm or receiving some help to become established as the owner of a produce store, he didn't hesitate. The year was 1928, my twin brother Rudolf and I had just been born, and our parents were already 35. . . .

My brother Rudolf and I were six weeks old when my parents established their business in Oberhausen, a large city in the grimy industrial heartland of Germany, the Ruhr. My grandmother, whose six remaining children were all adults, persuaded my parents to leave me behind "temporarily," especially since Rudolf was still frail from a hernia operation. With this move, my grandmother, the undisputed matriarch of the family, separated us for good, for she had not the slightest intention of returning me to my parents. After three years of pleading, my mother gave up because my father never encouraged her. He believed I was much better off on the farm.

I must have been four years old when I first remember meeting my mother. She scooped me up in her arms, broke into uncontrollable sobs and covered my face with kisses. Deeply embarrassed, I tore myself loose and ran toward my grandmother. It must have broken my mother's heart, for to me, my grandmother was my mother. It was a mutually deep and abiding love.

The tough and decisive woman adored me, and I was very much aware of my good fortune. While Rudolf grew up in an apartment in the grimiest area of Germany, I was raised on a prosperous farm by a woman who was eager to give me every social and educational opportunity.

My brother did have one marked advantage, however. While my grandparents were indifferent to politics and approved of Hitler and his regime only because of his economic success, my father hated the Nazis with an unrelenting fury, and he transmitted that to my brother with some success. Rudolf eventually joined the Hitler Youth, but not voluntarily as I had done.

A Violent Dislike

Like many disillusioned front line soldiers, my father had briefly joined the Communists after the armistice of 1918, partly because he despised most officers. He soon changed to the Social Democrats, perhaps out of deference to my grandmother who was a rigidly devout Catholic and couldn't stand the "heathen Bolsheviks." When my father and the Social Democrats fought the Nazis in pubs and on the streets, they were a rather forlorn band among a plethora of right wing groups. No sane person could have predicted that just 12 years later they would rule the nation. But the Nazis had long memories. My father was twice interrogated by the *Gestapo* about his early opposition. By then he was no longer a card-carrying Social Democrat, mainly because the party had become too fragmented. But to his credit, and unlike countless other Communists and Social Democrats, the Nazis could never persuade him to join their ranks. As a result, he was classified as "politically unreliable," a dangerous category indeed.

Since we lived 200 miles apart, I wasn't at first aware of my father's violent dislike of the regime. That was fortuitous for him; I eventually became such a fanatic disciple of the *Führer* [leader] that I might have turned in my own father if he had goaded me once too often. Luckily, we saw each other no more than twice a year when he returned to the farm to help with the harvest.

Indoctrination

By 1936, the glorious year in which our troops regained the Rhineland and Germany hosted the spectacular, successful

Olympic Games, I was eight, but already deeply under the spell of the new ideology. It's often assumed that our indoctrination began at ten, when we joined the *Jungvolk*, the junior branch of the Hitler Youth, for children 10 to 14. We did, at that age, become the political soldiers of the Third Reich, but our basic training had begun at six, when we entered elementary school. For me that year was 1933, three months after the aging and near-senile President Paul von Hindenburg reluctantly appointed Hitler the Chancellor, believing that only his NSDAP (*Nationalsozialistische Deutsche Arbeiterpartei*) [Nazi party] was strong enough to contain the Communists. Besides, Hitler, as the leader of the party with most members in the *Reichstag* [Parliament], adamantly refused to accept anything less than the chancellorship and threatened to boycott all parliamentary functions. The disunity of the other parties made his threat effective. The opposition dismantled itself before Hitler did.

Unlike our elders, we five- and six-year-olds knew nothing of the freedom, the turmoil and the death throes of the Weimar Republic [the German government after World War I]. We had

The Hitler Youth movement emphasized activism, physical training, Nazi ideology, and absolute obedience to Hitler.

never heard the bracing tones of public dissent, let alone opposition. We just went to school. My first teacher was *Herr* Becker, former company commander in World War I, super patriot and strict disciplinarian who, in the first three months, wholeheartedly embraced the new guidelines imposed by the Nazis. The Law Against Overcrowding of German Schools was put in effect on April 7, 1933. In imposing a quota system, it was specifically directed at the Jews.

More than any other political party, the NSDAP recognized that those who control the children own the future. We swallowed our daily dose of nationalistic instruction as naturally as our morning milk. Soon the portrait of Hitler hung harmonically on the same wall with the crucifix, as the saviour who had restored Germany's dignity and pride. Even in working democracies, children are too immature and dependent to question the veracity of what they are taught. That should be the task of aware parents. Most of our elders failed us because they themselves were captivated by the new spirit.

Herr Becker, the good Party member and pious Catholic, (not an unusual combination in the overwhelmingly Catholic Rhineland), was most influential in forming our picture of the world. Even before it became the official government policy to discriminate against the Jews, he had told us they were "different."

This prejudice, shared by millions of Germans, turned often to hatred after the promulgation of the Nuremberg Racial Laws of September 1935. Henceforth, Jews were no longer legal German citizens, but members of an inferior, alien race despite their impressive achievements. *Herr* Becker demonstrated in his weekly "racial science" instruction how and why they were different. We absorbed his demented views as matter-of-factly as if he were teaching arithmetic. "If their noses are shaped like an upside down 6," he declared, "they are usually Jewish, although some of these telltale signs have become hidden by their unfortunate mixing with our pure blood."

When I asked my grandmother what this mixing of blood meant, she looked at me with some consternation. "Well," she said finally, "it's like taking a cow to a strange bull to get a different kind of calf."

"That's good, isn't it?" I asked, aware that we had three different breeds of milk cows. "It is," she said, "but apparently this bunch wants to stick to the same bull."

In the late summer of 1936, after my grandfather and I had been glued to the radio during the Olympic Games, he had fallen asleep outside and contracted pneumonia. Ten days later my Aunt Maria woke me in the middle of the night. "Come and say good-bye to your *Grossvater*," she said, tears rolling down her cheeks. He still clutched his pipe when I saw him for the last time in his huge poster bed. His white beard was clean of all soup stains and his face was deadly pale. A terrible cough shook his body, but suddenly his eyes focused on me and he smiled. My aunt shoved me closer and he fumbled for my hand. "Don't give any more *Schnapps* [liquor] to the chickens, you little bum," he croaked, "or I'll . . ." He never finished the sentence. . . .

A School Friend

Herr Becker was an effective teacher, partly because of the terror he evoked in us. If you did not do your homework, you'd better have padded your leather shorts with newspaper, although *Herr* Becker was wise to that and sometimes caned our open palms. But when a less intelligent pupil tried, he showed him a condescending kind of mercy, citing Goethe, "Against stupidity, even the Gods battle in vain." By 1936, I had become one of *Herr* Becker's favorites, since I learned with ease. But our introduction had been shaky because of my association with Heinz Ermann.

Heinz was the first friend of my childhood. His parents owned a cattle business just up the street from us, and we had taken an immediate liking to each other in kindergarten. *Frau* Ermann was very generous with cookies and I usually followed Heinz home. I was impressed by his Uncle Siegfried's wooden leg, a remembrance of the 1914 Battle of the Sommes, where he had earned the Iron Cross I. Class for conspicuous bravery. Uncle Siegfried taught us how to ride and wasn't above playing marbles with us, something my uncles would never have done. Uncle Siegfried was proud of his service for the Fatherland. But the new Fatherland wasn't proud of him. Just 13 years after he had shown me how to saddle a horse properly, Siegfried and most members of the Ermann family were gassed in Auschwitz for being Jewish "subhumans."

Although the Law Against Overcrowding of German Schools was already in effect, Heinz and I started school together. But within weeks, he and two other Jewish children were ostracized by *Herr* Becker, who made it clear to us that these classmates were "different." He didn't harass them, he never whipped them, he just ignored them. The three sat forlornly on a bench in a corner, which the teacher sneeringly designated as "Palestine."

"It'll Soon Pass"

During a recess when I played with Heinz as we had done in kindergarten, *Herr* Becker pulled me to one side and hissed, "Good German boys don't play with Jews." I was bewildered. Was Heinz no longer a German? When I asked my grandmother, she became angry. "Of course Heinz is a German. I'll talk to *Herr* Becker about this nonsense."

I never knew whether she did, for within a week the issue became moot. The Jewish children were "transferred" to their own school in a room of the synagogue. When I brought up the subject again, my grandmother was embarrassed, something I had never seen before. "Listen, boy," she said, "it has something to do with the Ermanns not being Catholic. We have a new government now that thinks Jews shouldn't be with you Catholic kids. It'll soon pass and you can play with Heinz again."

There was widespread anti-Semitism throughout Germany long before Hitler came to power, although the half million Jews (less than one percent of our population) had become remarkably well assimilated. The exceptions were the *Ostjuden*, the East European Jews, largely impoverished and ostracized by the successful native German Jews. Many prosperous Jews, in fact, advocated closing the borders to them. The 20 percent or so who comprised the *Ostjuden* were, they reasoned, too visible and likely to incite more discrimination. When the Nazis came to power, though, most Jews buried their internal dissension and closed ranks against their now hostile government.

An Abiding Obsession

The Jews, primarily liberals who had supported the Weimar Republic, knew they were going to face tough times, but only a demented prophet of doom could have foreseen their terrible fate.

For the past 14 years, Hitler had blamed them for every misfortune that had befallen Germany, especially the country's defeat in World War I. This, he claimed, had been triggered by Jew-inspired Leftist radicals on the home front. Many optimists believed he would moderate once he legitimately headed the government. These, after all, were not the Middle Ages. Many influential leaders of the well-organized Jewish community counseled that there was no reason for panic. They were dead wrong. Hitler changed his mind on many issues, but never on the "Jewish Question." His hatred of all Jews remained an abiding, all-consuming obsession to his last breath.

The common man's dislike of Jews ranged from non-existent to violent, but not even rabid Nazis yet advocated their deaths. There was an element of envy which Hitler cleverly exploited, for the Jews were seen as the economically privileged class which had not suffered as much during the '20s. There was some truth in that since nearly half the Jews of Germany who were gainfully employed, had their own businesses. A disproportionately high percentage of physicians and attorneys were Jewish, so when Hitler almost immediately excluded Jews from practicing law, his measure was widely applauded. Even my grandmother agreed that there were too many "blood-sucking" lawyers around, but she included the Gentile ones. Most farmers worth anything were always in one litigation or another over land or livestock.

Remnants of Past Centuries

In Catholic provinces like the Rhineland and Bavaria, religious intolerance was a remnant of centuries of persecution by the church. Some form of dislike was almost respectable, and all Catholic children were taught that the Jews had killed Christ. In my own family, I had overheard remarks which sounded anti-Semitic, although my grandmother remained friends with *Frau* Ermann and lit her Sabbath fire to the day of their deportation.

"*Du dummer Narr*," she once chided my Uncle Franz when he had bought a calf from *Herr* Ermann without haggling. "He is a Jew, and if you don't try to beat him down he considers you dumb." This was a statement of fact, and had nothing to do with intolerance.

Wittlich being the county seat and major trade center within 50 kilometers, had a fairly sizable Jewish population, about 250. Jews came from smaller towns to worship in the stately 1910 synagogue. In the early years, the few open acts of hostility against the Jews were perpetrated by outside Nazis. Most demonstrations were day-long boycotts by brown-shirted storm troopers who displayed signs with warnings like, "Good Germans don't buy from Jews." Some customers like my Aunt Maria paid no attention, but many did, since the troopers asked the customers for their names. In any small town it was much harder to be a Jew; there was no anonymity. When Jews were forced to display the yellow star on their clothing after September 1941, no place afforded them anonymity. By then, the Jews of Wittlich were long gone.

A Good-bye

One afternoon Heinz came to our farm, dressed in his best velvet suit, to say good-bye. "My Uncle Herbert is taking me with him for a while," he said, but with no enthusiasm. Uncle Herbert was a rabbi in, I believe, Cologne. "It'll be nice for you to see a big city," said my grandmother. She gave each of us a big piece of cake, usually only a Sunday treat. We shook hands awkwardly. "*Auf Wiedersehen, Frau* Heck," he said, but just nodded to me. She smoothed his hair and put her arm around his shoulder, which was quite a display of affection for her. "I think it'll be better this way, Heinz."

Maybe my grandmother sensed it would be better for both of us. Our friendship, which never had a chance to mature, could not have withstood the pressure of disapproval by the state. I already felt a sense of relief at Heinz' departure. I had never included Heinz and his family with the Jewish "traitors" who, with the Bolsheviks, were determined to do us in, but I never mentioned his name either, particularly when I was asked in Hitler Youth character interviews if I had ever associated with a Jew. Moreover, I readily admitted that I considered my father a misguided former Social Democrat who was too stupid to grasp our new order. Instinctively I realized that such an admission would not hurt my career: it was a measure of one's dedication to prevail against parental hostility.

First Communion

In 1937, Rudolf and I celebrated our First Holy Communion, a three-day festival on which my grandmother spent more money than her daughter's wedding. I remembered Heinz then, only because he sent me a card of congratulation. It was the first summer that Rudi and I had spent together, and the instruction leading up to the First Communion took three months. We were the only twins that year and my grandmother insisted we should be together for this momentous event, so Rudi came from Oberhausen where he lived with my parents. As usual, nobody asked my mother. Rudi and I were difficult to tell apart, particularly in our summer attire—leather shorts and a shirt. To ease the identity problem, my grandmother had Rudi's hair cut a little shorter which worked until I took the scissors to mine! We were highly competitive, and a bit too much for one family.

At the end of that summer, I visited Oberhausen for the first time with my Aunt Luise. So impressed was I by the huge city, the fire-belching steel plants, the clanging street cars and the chance to go to the movies, that I tolerated my mother's frequent kisses. Even my father was pleased when I admired his three-story-high steam shovel.

A Spat with Father

Disaster struck on the third evening when my mother served my favorite beverage, a cup of cocoa. I made a face and my father looked up from his dinner. "What's the matter?" he asked. "Doesn't our young gentleman like his cocoa?" His sarcasm made me reckless. "On the farm, we wouldn't serve this kind of milk to the pigs," I said, and found myself sitting on the floor. My father had knocked me off my chair with a swift backhand. What I would have tolerated from my uncles, I couldn't take from my father. Stunned, I got up from the floor. "I'm going home tomorrow morning," I announced. My mother began to wail, "It's all right, child. I'll make you another cup."

"Like hell you will," yelled my father. "I'll be damned if I'll cater to a nine-year-old punk." Wildly, he shook his fist at me. "You have all the makings of an arrogant Nazi." He went to work at six o'clock the next morning, and we boarded the eight o'clock express for Koblenz. My aunt was so angry she kicked me when

I asked her to buy me a bottle of lemonade. "Drink water, you spoiled *Schwein*," she hissed, "you just ruined my summer vacation. Now it's back to the grind, thanks to you."

Far from being angry, my grandmother chuckled with glee when my aunt told her why we had returned so soon. "I just knew he couldn't stand that dump for two full weeks," she said, "and he's right about their milk; it isn't fit for our pigs." That encounter set the tone of my relationship with my father until the end of the war, for the next year I did the unforgivable in his eyes: I voluntarily joined the *Jungvolk*. When he first saw me in uniform on one of his brief visits to the farm, he couldn't contain himself. "They're going to bury you in that monkey suit, *Du verdammter Idiot*," he shouted, but I looked coldly through him and walked away. I had just returned from the most soulshaking event of my life and was beyond his petty venom.

Craving Action

When I was sworn into the *Jungvolk* on April 20, 1938, Hitler's 49th birthday, I had no idea I would attend the Nuremberg Party Congress, the annual *Reichsparteitag*—high mass of Nazism—that fall. Far from being forced, my peers and I could hardly wait to join the Hitler Youth. We craved action, which was offered in abundance. There was the monotonous drill, but that could be endured for the opportunity to hike, camp, enact war games in the field, and play a variety of sports. All these activities were designed to make us fit according to our motto: swift as greyhounds, tough as leather and hard as the steel of Krupp. In that, the Hitler Youth succeeded. In *The Rise and Fall of the Third Reich*, author William L. Shirer noted that Germany was filled with superbly fit children, always marching and singing. Our prewar activities resembled those of the Boy Scouts, but with much more emphasis on discipline and political indoctrination. The paraphernalia, the parades, the flags and the symbols, the soul-stirring music and the pomp and mysticism were very close in feeling to religious rituals.

When I raised three fingers of my right hand to the sky in the oath to the *Führer*, my left gripping the flag of my unit, my spine tingled in the conviction that I now belonged to something both majestic and threatened by bitter enemies. It was *Deutschland*.

"I promise in the Hitler Youth to do my

duty at all times in love and faithfulness to help the Führer—so help me God."

"Blood and Honor"

As the final act of the induction ceremony, we were handed the dagger with the Swastika inlaid in the handle and the inscription "Blood and Honor" on its blade. On that cool, windy April afternoon, I accepted the two basic tenets of the Nazi creed: belief in the innate superiority of the Germanic-Nordic race, and the conviction that total submission to Germany and to the *Führer* was our first duty.

My attendance that year at the Nuremberg Party Congress hinged on a promise to my grandmother that I would enter the *Cusanus Gymnasium* [secondary school] to study for the priesthood. Normally delegates were carefully selected and limited to the older members, but the district had been ordered to include even 10-year-olds that year, if they could afford the 25 marks for the trip. Although that was a week's wages for the average worker, it was a bargain since it included transportation, all meals and a bunk in the immense tent city Camp Langwasser. Nuremberg, the medieval showcase of Germany, was the ideal location for the congress with its super nationalistic appeal. Austria had been annexed that year, with the enthusiastic approval of most Austrians, and the theme of the congress was "Greater Germany."

On Saturday, September 10, the "Day of the Hitler Youth," I stood in the first row of the immense stadium, facing the twin grandstands, where huge Swastikas were held in the grip of granite eagles. The tension ran high among us 80,000 lined up in rows as long as the entire stadium, each 12 boys or girls deep.

"Tempo and Intensity"

The *Reichsführer* of the Hitler Youth, Baldur von Schirach, whose mother was an American, made a short, flowery and forgettable speech, and then introduced Hitler. We greeted him with a thunderous triple *"Sieg Heil,"* and it took all of our discipline to end it there, as we had been instructed. My knees were shaking, and when the *Führer* beamed down on us, his eyes caught mine—I was absolutely sure of that, as was every other one of my comrades. Then he began to speak quietly, almost conversationally, man to man. Soon, he increased both tempo and intensity, but occasionally returned to the slower pace, piquing us for the next crescendo. It was a sure-fire method which frequently mesmerized the non-believers and even his bitter foes. We never had a chance. I'm certain none of us took our eyes off him. We simply became an instrument in the hands of the supreme master.

Much later, in one of my postwar history classes, I had a teacher who had joined the Nazi Party in 1928, and was thus indicted as an "Old Fighter." When I asked him why he, as an educated adult, had fallen for the siren song, he smiled wistfully, "Hitler appealed to the atavistic instinct in us by not being afraid to shout out loud what we only silently admitted to ourselves—that we Germans were indeed the superior race."

That echoed exactly my feelings at the closing of Hitler's speech. His right fist punctuated the air in a staccato of short, powerful jabs as he roared out a promise and an irresistible enticement of power already proven to the world. "You, my youth," he shouted, with his eyes seemingly fixed only on me, "are our nation's most precious guarantee for a great future, and you are destined to be the leaders of a glorious new world order under the supremacy of National Socialism." From that moment on, I belonged to Adolf Hitler body and soul.

Propaganda and Cultural Control

CHAPTER 3

Chapter Preface

Propaganda was an important tool used by the Nazi regime to maintain control and impose order in Germany during the 1930s and 1940s. The government of Nazi Germany was among the first in the world to use the arts and powerful technological means to speedily publicize its messages to a large number of people.

The idea of using the arts to build enthusiasm for the goals of powerful classes did not originate with the Nazis or stop with them. However, the Nazis innovatively used the new media of film and radio, along with other technologically advanced means, to effectively inspire masses of citizens to support their aims. Using these media, the Nazi message reached a larger number of citizens more rapidly than it would have using older techniques.

For example, the Nazi Party supported filmmaker Leni Riefenstahl, who produced awe-inspiring, pro-Nazi films such as *Triumph of the Will* and *Olympia*, a paean to the 1936 Olympic Games, which were held in Berlin. Although Riefenstahl's movies are widely recognized as visually stunning and technically masterful early classics, the films she made for the Nazis are reviled because they glorified a government whose policies were later clearly seen to be abhorrent.

The work of other modern artists has been used by governments to build enthusiasm for their policies. The creations of Soviet filmmaker Sergei Eisenstein and U.S. musician Bruce Springsteen were appropriated by politicians to inspire the populace with progovernment messages. Yet Riefenstahl and others allied with the Nazis were unique among modern artists in the degree to which they embraced their government's aims. Riefenstahl's films were directly financed by Nazi government sources, and she was closely associated with Adolf Hitler and Nazi propaganda minister Joseph Goebbels. And because of the Nazi government's atrocities, when Riefenstahl died at the age of 101—over half a century after she made her pro-Nazi films—*Los Angeles Times* entertainment reporter Reed Johnson wrote that "her work will forever be tainted with the stench of the death camps."

Similarly, the architect Albert Speer worked as an official Nazi government planner and designer. He created structures, lighting, and ceremonies for Nazi mass meetings and rallies that built so much enthusiasm among participants that the events were likened to stirring religious rituals. The style of Speer's creations was similar to that of other designers whose pompous, colossal work was emblematic of non-Nazi governments. Yet because of Speer's close association with the Nazi government and its malevolent policies, he has been judged morally culpable of helping to build enthusiasm for a corrupt cause.

Garnering support among the populace was a primary aim of Nazi publicity efforts. But leaders did not stop at such positive tactics. They also used publicity in overtly negative ways to get public support—by instilling fear and hatred among the citizenry.

For example, in the early 1930s when the Nazis first came to power, they publicized the new concentration camps they had opened to hold the thousands of loosely defined criminals and political enemies they arrested. The many newspaper stories generated by the Nazi Party about the camps characterized them positively as centers where inmates would be educated and instilled with values promoting hard work. The accounts trumpeted Nazi success in ridding society of criminal elements. But there was no mistaking the sinister side of propaganda about detention camps. Its negative intent was clear: to cow the rest of the population into fearing that the same thing could happen to anyone who disagreed with the government, refused to hold a regular job, was promiscuous, or committed any number of questionable offenses.

Likewise, Nazi publicity efforts aimed to build hatred against certain groups and thus cement support for the party. Besides promoting hatred of criminals and political enemies, the Nazis developed propaganda to build upon the anti-Semitism that already existed in Germany.

Although the handful of obviously anti-Semitic dramas by Nazi-sponsored filmmakers were so crude and vile that they were box-office failures, the Nazis produced a stream of short newsreel films that were the German people's sole visual source of information about the outside world. (Starting in 1939, Germans were forbidden to listen to foreign newscasts.) These short films generally accompanied showings of regular entertainment movies, and they were peppered with anti-Semitism. Nazi propagandists, through film, radio, and the press, excoriated the supposed strong influence of Jews on foreign governments and presented Jews unfavorably, claiming they were responsible for Germany's economic problems and even for World War II.

Many Germans later said they did not share the anti-Semitism of the Nazis or were even embarrassed by it. Still, there seems to be little doubt that the barrage of official, negative propaganda promoting hatred of Jews and other marginal groups tapped a jingoistic undercurrent in German culture and generated a great deal of momentum for the party. Thus, the Nazis' use of fear-based public relations and more positive types of propaganda enabled leaders to carry out their policies, which ranged from economic improvement measures to large-scale persecution of reviled groups.

The Propaganda Apparatus

Joseph Goebbels

The Nazi regime relied on propaganda to win the support of the German people. The person in charge of the propaganda effort was Joseph Goebbels, Hitler's Minister for Propaganda and Popular Enlightenment. Goebbels kept a diary that reveals how he used radio, film, art, newspapers, and brute force to build a cooperative public. Goebbels also battled to present a favorable spin on Germany's actions in the foreign press. His account reflects his intellectual abilities, his anti-Jewish opinions, his sentimentalism toward children, and his hero-worship of Hitler. These selections begin as Germany has just made its first outright war move (the blitzkrieg invasion of Poland), Britain has declared war against Germany, and German submarines have begun sinking British ships. Goebbels records his and others' reaction to many events, including the 1939 assassination attempt on Hitler. Goebbels, his wife, and his six children committed suicide as Berlin was invaded by enemy armies in 1945.

16 October 1939 (Monday)

[B]ritish statesman] Lloyd George has written another article in the Hearst press containing violent attacks on the British government. Very advantageous for us. I order it to be published without too much fuss, however, so as not to compromise L.G.

I deal with a series of investigations undertaken in co-operation with [security official Reinhard] Heydrich. A small group of defeatists in artistic circles. I have them rounded up straight away.

The children are here. I spend a wounderful hour with the little ones. We gather chestnuts in the garden. A pleasure.

In the afternoon I attend a request concert for the Wehrmacht [armed forces]. I make a profound impression there. Donate

---

Joseph Goebbels, *The Goebbels Diaries: 1939–1941*, edited and translated by Fred Taylor. New York: G.P. Putnam's Sons, 1982. Copyright © 1982 by Fred Taylor and Hamish Hamilton Ltd. All rights reserved. Reproduced by permission.

1500 people's wireless receivers [radio sets produced by the Nazi régime for mass-distribution] for the front.

Work at home. The torpedoing of the *Royal Oak* is a bare-knuckle blow at England's prestige.

Fander tells me about a crazy business he has heard of. I get the Gestapo to step in straight away to make an example.

Mother, Ursel and Axel here. We chat . . .

17 October 1939 (Tuesday)

Yesterday: Renewed savage attacks against [British leader Winston] Churchill. Propaganda plan against France drafted. A nice little propaganda pamphlet designed for the front. Harsh tone in the press against London. No more talk of peace. The High Command stops issuing reports about Poland. [Propaganda Ministry official Fritz] Hippler back from Poland with a lot of material for the Ghetto film.

English battleship *Repulse* is torpedoed by a German U-boat. England's black day. Poor Churchill.

Organisational questions with [labor official Robert] Ley. The problem of what to do with Warsaw. Best put under quarantine.

Kaufmann from the Hitler Youth delivers a report on propaganda, press and film work in the Hitler Youth. He will do his job well . . .

Führer [Hitler]: he is delighted with the magnificent achievements of our U-boats [submarines]. I show him some examples from my propaganda work. He is very pleased with them. Shaw has let loose a few more *bon mots* against Churchill. The Führer is very much amused.

The Führer describes the fragility of the former Hapsburg Empire. How the German element was neglected. The malevolent and strange character of [Hapsburg] Emperor Franz-Josef. The tragedy of [mysterious deaths in] Mayerling. The beautiful Empress. How he personally became an anti-Semite only in Vienna. How his father was anti-clerical. The great achievements of Lueger. I tell him about my preliminary work on the Jew-film, which interests him greatly. A report to him on our suppression of rumours. I intend to hand the whole business over to the People's Court [radical court the Nazis created to try people accused of criticizing the government]. . . .

21 October 1939 (Saturday)

The financial success of our films is altogether amazing. We are becoming real war profiteers. In the theatre as well, though not so pronounced . . .

. . . Shortage of salt in Berlin as a result of transportation difficulties. I quickly ensure relief . . .

. . . With the Führer: absolute quiet in the West. Absolutely nothing to report. I tell the Führer about our enormous success with the forces' request concerts, which pleases him greatly.

Duties, work, without a break. I am run-down and nervous. In the evening, a short visit to [wife] Magda in the clinic. She is relatively well again. I am so glad. Nothing must happen to her. We chat about all our worries.

We release the attack against Churchill. It will hit home . . .

22 October 1939 (Sunday)

Yesterday: Wonderful caricatures of me appear in the English newspapers. One could laugh oneself sick at them. International journalists are taken to the French prisoner-of-war camps. I intend to ferret out a few more lies.

Our attack against Churchill hit home. It has been taken up by the entire neutral press. The English lies are being noted in Paris, causing great ill-feeling and indignation. These days in London, all they do is tell lies.

The Ankara-London-Paris treaty is the talk of the world. An article in [Russian newspaper] *Izvestia*, inspired by Stalin, reproves the Turks and confirms German-Russian friendship in very clear terms. Extraordinarily valuable for us.

I read an address by a Professor of Theology named Fabrizius. It is bare-faced treason. And the author boasts the protection of the Wehrmacht. A fellow like that should be strung up. A subversive in priest's clothing . . .

. . . Work at home. It is grey, rainy autumn.

In the evening, with the Führer. A reception for the [Nazi Party leaders] Reichsleiters and Gauleiters. All the good old comrades. We talk ourselves to a standstill. Best of moods.

The Führer speaks for two hours. Gives a picture of our military and economic superiority and our determination to win victory, by all means and with complete ruthlessness, if it comes to battle—which he now considers almost inevitable. We have no choice. And at the end lies the great, all-embracing German people's Reich. The Führer speaks very clearly and with great determination. And inspires everyone with renewed heart for the fight and belief in victory.

With such a Führer and such a Party leadership, we must and shall succeed. . . .

24 October 1939 (Tuesday)

We chat with the Führer about the changeableness of our conception of feminine beauty. What was considered beautiful forty years ago is now fat, plump, dumpy. Sport, gymnastics and the fight against sexual cant have changed people's attitudes, probably for the better. We are taking huge, swift strides towards a new classical age. And we are the trail-blazers of this revolution in all respects.

England intends to instal a new German government in London, including [exiled opponents] Rauschning, Treviranus, Wirth, and Brüning. A ridiculous, stupid, and childish plan. But I can believe anything of these idiots.

In the afternoon: censoring of photos and articles.

Magda is a little better again. I hope she can soon come home. Check the weekly newsreel and lay down guidelines for the text. Turned out well. Further problems with our Jew-film. Synagogue shots extraordinarily powerful. We are working on it at the moment, aiming to create a propaganda masterpiece from the welter of material. Afterwards discuss a further range of film problems with Hippler. Deep into the night. . . .

2 November 1939 (Thursday)

Newsreel completed. Turned out excellently. The Führer is also very pleased with it. Then new rushes from the Jew-film, which are also very effective. Then a propaganda film from Ufa about air defence, which tries a humorous approach, actually with great success. Script of the Poland film checked, and thoroughly revised and corrected.

The work never lets up, and at the moment it gives me huge pleasure.

In the evening, speak with Magda again about Harald. He is causing her some worries.

3 November 1939 (Friday)

Yesterday: All quiet in politics and the war.

The English White Book on our concentration camps is arousing some interest. I shall prepare two White Books to counter it: one on English colonial atrocities, and another about the lies of the English press. In this way, I shall neutralise the effect to a great extent.

[Soviet Foreign Minister Vyacheslav] Molotov's speech continues to enjoy a mixed reception. This is due to the English, who cannot rid themselves of the illusion that Moscow belongs on their side . . .

The Censor's Fist

The broadcasts of U.S. journalists from Nazi-controlled Berlin were highly censored. But William Shirer still managed to provide a glimpse of how Nazi propaganda masters in print and on the air tried to use distortion, threats, and entertainment to influence the German people. Here, Shirer reports on how Germany's invasion of Poland was depicted.

Berlin September 1, 1939

It's just quarter after one in the morning Berlin time, and we're half way through our first blackout. The city is completely darkened, and has been since seven o'clock. . . .

Behind the darkened windows the people sit in their homes and listen to the radio, which plays martial band music, or a stirring symphony from Beethoven or Brahms [celebrated German composers], and every once in a while you get a news announcement. . . .

The isolation that you feel from the outside world on a night like this is increased by a new decree issued tonight prohibiting the listening in to foreign broadcasts. From now on you can't listen to them. . . .

Now how, do you think, is this war being presented to the German people by the press tonight? In the first place the military operations are exclusively termed "a counter-attack" against Poland. Poland is held entirely to blame for what she is receiving, and England is held responsible for not making Poland accept what all the papers, and what indeed Herr Hitler described today in the Reichstag as "Germany's very generous offer to Warsaw".

William L. Shirer, *This is Berlin*. New York: Overlook, Peter Mayer Publishers, Inc., 1999, pp. 68–81.

... Press Conference: new moves against England prepared. All cultural contact with the Poles forbidden. Let them help themselves, and then we shall see how far they get ...

... A view of the current public mood. This is excellent ...

... With the Führer. I deliver a report on my trip to Poland, which he finds very interesting. In particular, my description of the Jewish problem meets with his complete approval. The Jew is a waste product. More a clinical than a social phenomenon. England's hirelings! We must bring this out much more in our propaganda.

The Jerry-Letter meets with the Führer's fullest approval. We consider whether it should be included along with the Zionist Protocols [forged documents giving an account of a Jewish "conspiracy" to destroy Christian civilisation] for our propaganda in France.

Question: should we release pictures of the destruction in Warsaw? Advantages and disadvantages. Advantage that of shock-effect. The Führer wants to see the pictures personally first. ...

7 November 1939 (Tuesday)

Yesterday: The London press carries on lying. Somewhat less so in Paris. England and France have considerable domestic difficulties.

We are also taking a harder line against the USA. Holland will also be cosseted no longer. It has published a weak-as-water Orange Book on England's piratical policy.

I restrict the import of foreign, particularly American films. The public does not want to see this stuff any more. In broadcasting, I place further limits on the activities of the smaller outlet stations. ...

8 November 1939 (Wednesday)

Yesterday: We use the press to take a harder line against Belgium, and in particular Holland, for the spinelessness of their neutrality policy so far as England is concerned. A little difficult to get it off the ground. But it works in the end. It will certainly attract a lot of notice.

The B.Z. [The *Berliner Zeitung*, a Berlin newspaper] has committed a serious political error for the second time. Editor dismissed.

I instruct that our attacks on France and England should be

targeted a little more realistically. The German people must not believe that defeating them is child's play. We must not become defeatist, but we must also resist spreading illusionism. For my part, I am convinced that England's position and her power are both weaker than ever before.

The craziest rumours are circulating throughout the country about what will happen next. At the moment I am in no position to do much about this. ...

9 November 1939 (Thursday)

Yesterday: A beautiful autumn day. Everyone is tense with expectation in view of the Führer's coming decisions. In the meantime, the political situation has become somewhat fluid again. The peace appeal by the Belgian and Dutch monarchs has been contemptuously rejected in Paris and London. This spares us the work of rejecting it ourselves. The German press took little notice of the appeal, and made no comment. Anxiety is growing in Holland and Belgium. We no longer bother to deny all the rumours that are buzzing about. This is also a tactic, and an infamous one at that.

The Comintern [Communist International group] has issued an impertinent statement, appealing to the proletarian masses against the 'warmongering bourgeoisie'. The same old tone. Despite everything, this alliance with Moscow can give one a slightly eerie feeling . . .

. . . We prepare the public for the clothing ration cards that will soon be coming, and ensure that there will be no rush on stocks of textile goods, leading to empty shops.

Flight to Munich. On the way, read the script for the film *Jud Süss*. [Jud Süss was the name of a fictional, depraved Jewish character.]. (. . .) Turned out very well. The first genuine anti-Semitic film . . .

In the evening, to the Bürgerbräukeller [hall]. The old comrades [from a 1923 uprising]! Many are missing, many appear in field-grey uniform. The Führer is greeted with unimaginable enthusiasm. In his speech he delivers a biting attack on England. Searing attacks on the banditry of British policy. We shall never surrender. Vows five years of war. And England will get a taste of our weapons.

Wild enthusiasm rages through the hall. This speech will be a world-sensation.

Travel back to Berlin with the Führer immediately after his speech. . . .

At Nuremberg comes bad news. There the Führer is handed a telegram, according to which an explosion took place at the Bürgerbräu hall shortly after he left. Eight dead, sixty injured. The whole roof crashed down. At first the Führer thinks this must be a mistake. I check with Berlin, and the entire report is correct. There had been unsuccessful attempts to stop the train. The extent of the damage is enormous. An assassination attempt, doubtless cooked up in London and probably carried out by Bavarian separatists.

The Führer dictates a communiqué, which I issue straight away in Nuremberg. We give thorough consideration to the probable culprits, consequences, and the measures to be taken. We shall restrain the masses until we at least know from where the attempt came. The Führer and the rest of us have escaped death by a miracle. If the meeting had gone according to the programme, as every other year, then we would all no longer be living. In contrast to earlier years, the Führer started half an hour earlier and finished before time. He stands under the protection of the Almighty. He will die only when his mission has been fulfilled.

The police in Munich obviously failed in its task. The necessary precautions were not taken. There will doubtless be consequences. From now on, we telephone Munich from every station on the way. But the picture does not change during the night. When we catch the culprits, the punishment will fit the enormity of the crime.

We stay awake right through the night. I set the entire news apparatus in Berlin in motion. This time, we shall not perish in silence.

An hour of sleep. Then immediately back to my post.

10 November 1939 (Friday)

Yesterday: Arrival in Berlin. [Hermann] Göring and [Hans] Lammers waiting for the Führer's train at the station. The Führer is very strong and erect.

A few clues have been discovered. But they point in no particular direction. It could not have been prepared without the co-operation of the Bürgerbräu staff. A reward of 100,000 marks has been offered for the culprits' apprehension.

Immediately to the Press Conference: I give the facts of the case and issue precise guidelines for the way the case should be handled. The reporting of the assassination attempt in Paris and London is contemptible. As is their custom, they are trying to push the responsibility on to us. But to counter this, I am mobilising the power of the entire German press. The masses want to assemble on the Wilhelmsplatz, but at the Führer's wish I head off any moves in that respect. The November day is grey and dull.

To work. The Führer's speech has been totally obliterated by the news of the bomb-attack so far as the foreign press is concerned.

With the Führer. We go through the entire assassination attempt once more. The number of clues as to the culprits' identities is mounting. But there are still no clear leads. And so we hold back our address to the people. First we must have the culprits. Then it will be unleashed. Himmler's inquiries are very wide-ranging. We have to believe that we shall catch the culprits.

On the Führer's instructions, I call off the Day of National Solidarity. In these times, it is too dangerous. We must conserve and protect our strength, for we shall have need of them during these critical hours.

A lot of work at home. The world press huffs and puffs. But we shall soon sort them out.

[British Prime Minister Neville] Chamberlain, who is ill, lets [British official Sir John] Simon reply to the Dutch-Belgian offer of mediation. A holding action. They have to continue to think about it. They will spend so long thinking that they'll get a smack in the eye.

In the evening, complete work on the weekly newsreel. On the Führer's instructions, we shall re-edit.

Spend a long time talking things over with Magda. We have so many money worries.

11 November 1939 (Saturday)

Yesterday: The Bürgerbräu assassination attempt still the big world-wide sensation. London and Paris are trying to push the blame on to us, as they did with the Reichstag [Parliament building] fire. We counter this energetically. The morale in the country is excellent. Still no sign of the culprits. A few small indications are coming to light.

Complete quiet in the West. But Holland is living in fear and anxiety. The same for Belgium. Twilight of the neutrals.

I give the press precise instructions. I speak about propaganda films and their methods. They are all too contrived and complicated. We expect too much of the people, and because of this they frequently find us completely incomprehensible. I urge a more primitive approach in our entire propaganda.

Again ban a number of foreign newspapers. They are ruining my entire mood. Even when they dress themselves up as pro-German.

The Triumph of National Socialism

Adolf Hitler

Among the most effective propaganda tools used by the Nazi regime were the image and voice of Adolf Hitler. Hitler was a prolific speaker; it is estimated that he made over fifteen hundred speeches, some of which were four hours long. New radio technology enabled the speeches to be broadcast far and wide. Hitler often delivered his speeches at rallies attended by large numbers of military and Hitler Youth marching and standing in formation. The large crowds, along with banners and other military regalia were orchestrated to inculcate a spirit of unity and support for Hitler. This atmosphere, combined with Hitler's intense, passionate speaking style, succeeded in winning over many converts.

The speech selected here was made in 1936, about four years after the Nazis came to power and only a month after the much-heralded opening of the Olympics in Berlin. The occasion was the Nazi party's annual convention in Nuremberg, and Hitler trumpeted familiar themes: economic progress, the heroism of Germany under the National Socialist party, the degeneracy of Germany's opponents, and the Jews as enemies.

"As we open this 'congress of honor,' we are stirred by two emotions, first, one of pride as we look back on the last four years, especially the last year, and, secondly, a feeling of the justification of all our acts as we behold the world about us filled with dissension and instability.

"Elsewhere years, if not decades, in the life of a nation pass without claiming especial consideration except where they involve political and economic collapse, and it is in this connection that we National Socialists proudly assert that the period of Germany's collapse dating from November, 1918, moved at a slower

---

Adolf Hitler, *Adolf Hitler: My New Order*, edited by Raoul de Roussy de Sales. New York: Reynal & Hitchcock, 1941. Copyright © 1941 by Reynal and Hitchcock, Inc. All rights reserved. Reproduced by permission.

pace than the period that marks the four years of our national recovery.

"Was this miracle a genuine revolution or was it not? Have our achievements justified it in the eyes of the German people and, above all, who else but us could have accomplished this wonder. . . ."

"What, however, has Nazism made of Germany in these four years? Which of our opponents would have the insolence to appear as a complainant against us today?

"What appeared in my proclamation of 1933 to be fantastic and impossible now appears a mere modest announcement of accomplishments that tower above it.

"Our opponents did not believe it possible that time would accomplish that program of 1933, which now looks so small to us. What would they have said, however, if I had presented to them that program which Nazism has genuinely accomplished in the last four years?

Trumpeting Economic Gains

"How they would have laughed if I had declared on January 30, 1933, that in four years Germany would have reduced its unemployment from six to one million;

"That the forced sale of peasant holdings would have been brought to an end;

"That the income of German agrarian economy would be higher than in any preceding year in our peace time;

"That the total national income would have risen from 41,000,000,000 marks to 56,000,000,000;

"That the German middle class and the German trades would experience a new period of prosperity;

"That commerce would regain its feet;

"That the German Hanseatic cities would no longer resemble ship cemeteries;

"That in 1936 ships totaling 640,000 tons would be under construction at German wharfs;

"That a multitude of factories would not double but triple and quadruple their employees;

"That many other new factories would appear;

"That the Krupp works would again hear the rumble of machines working for Germany's regeneration;

"That all these undertakings would recognize that their final law was service to the nation and not unscrupulous private profit;

"That inactive automobile factories would not only come to life again but would be greatly increased in size;

"That our production of automobiles of all sorts would increase from 45,000 in 1932 to almost 250,000 now;

"That in these four years the deficits of our cities and provinces would disappear;

"That the Reich would have a tax income increase of about 5,000,000,000 marks yearly;

"That the Reichsbank would finally be made financially sound;

"That its trains would be the fastest in the world;

"That the German Reich would receive roads such as had never been built since human culture existed;

"That of 7,000 kilometers [about 4,350 miles] of roads projected 1,000 would be in use after only four years and 4,000 more would be under construction;

"That tremendous new homestead colonies with hundreds of thousands of houses would appear in the Reich;

With his powerful oratory skills, Hitler was able to arouse great passion in his listeners. Here, a large crowd is gathered to hear him speak.

"That new buildings would rise which are among the largest in the world;

"That hundred upon hundreds of new immense bridges would cross valleys and gulleys;

Cultural Triumphs

"That German culture in such and like accomplishments would demonstrate its internal character;

"That the German theater would experience a renaissance;

"That the German people would take an active part in the revival of the drama;

"That Germany would experience a great intellectual awakening without a single Jew having a hand in it;

"That the German press would work only in the interests of Germany;

"That new professional ethics would be proclaimed for German business;

"That the German human being would experience a thorough reformation of his modes of activity and his character. . . ."

"What would our opponents have said if four years ago I would have predicted that four years hence the German people would be a united nation with neither Social Democrats, Communists, Centrists nor bourgeois parties left to transgress against the German people or trade unions to scatter dissension among the workers?

German Unity Touted

"What would they have said had I then predicted that four years hence there would no longer be independent states with their own legislatures and sixteen different flags and traditions, but that the whole nation from the humblest worker up to the soldier would be pledged to one flag?

"But, above all things, what would our opponents have said had I then prophesied that during these four years Germany would have shaken off the chains of the slavery of Versailles [a punishing treaty imposed on Germany after World War I], that the Reich would have regained its defense freedom, that, as formerly in peace time, every German would dedicate two years of his life to the freedom of his country, that our coasts and our

> ## Flames of Fanaticism
>
> *In 1933, Nazi propaganda chief Joseph Goebbels gave a speech at a huge book burning at a Berlin university.*
>
> At German universities, . . . few voices of protest were heard. Many university professors saw in national socialism the "*Volk* community" [community of the people] and "organic leadership" about which they had theorized in their courses for years. Noted professors like the philosopher Martin Heidegger, the art historian Wilhelm Pinder, and the surgeon Ferdinand Sauerbruch signed their names to proclamations and declarations of loyalty. The German Student Association, trying to compete with the National Socialist Student League, had elected a Nazi to lead it as early as July 1931. In April 1933 the Association now approached a representative of the Propaganda Ministry [headed by Joseph Goebbels] requesting support for a "symbolic" burning of "subversive writings"—by Jewish, Marxist, or other "non-German" authors. . . .
>
> When Goebbels arrived [for the Berlin book burning] at the Opernplatz in an open car, it was around midnight, and at that hour bonfires were blazing in many German university towns. Goebbels seemed "not particularly enthusiastic." Nonetheless, at the beginning of his address he proclaimed the end of an "era of Jewish hyperintellectualism." In the flames of twenty thousand burning books he saw the "intellectual basis of the November republic" being consumed.
>
> Ralf Georg Reuth, *Goebbels*. New York: Harcourt Brace, 1990, pp. 182–83.

commerce would be protected by a navy now in the course of construction, that a powerful new air weapon would vouchsafe protection to our cities and factories, and that the Rhineland would again be restored to the sovereignty of the Reich?

"And perchance what would these opponents have said had I predicted that before even four years had elapsed this National Socialist policy for the recovery of our honor and national freedom would received an affirming endorsement by ninety-nine per cent of the German electorate? . . ."

Castigating Enemies

"But a second miracle, and one which cannot fail to fill us with grim satisfaction, is the realization that our other predictions have proved all too true.

"Unrest, hate, and mistrust fill the world about us. With the exception of one major Power and a few other States, we encounter throughout Europe the convulsions of bolshevistic rioting and revolution.

"My party comrades, did it not strike you as something akin to symbolism that at a time when in other countries hate reigned and ruin spread there could take place in Berlin amid the plaudits of a happy people an Olympic festival dedicated to the noble motives of enlightened humanity?

"Despite all their attempts, it was not possible for even Jewish reporters to distort the truth and misrepresent what millions had seen with their own eyes."

"But while these Jewish-bolshevistic baiters and revolution mongers talked and showed a preference for applying an incendiary torch to human culture, National Socialist Germany, through heroic efforts and within its own frontiers and the restricted scope of its domestic resources has striven to rehabilitate its national economy, protect the lives of its people, and insure its economic future.

"The worries and disappointments that the government of the German people have encountered in this process in the last four years were probably greater and more acute than those that had confronted other governments in half a century. . . ."

Two Jewish Musicians Under the Nazi Regime

Martin Goldsmith

In 2000, National Public Radio commentator Martin Goldsmith published a memoir about the escape of his musician parents from their home in Nazi Germany. Goldsmith said he wrote the story to try to explain the "hole in my heart" that was created because his Jewish parents had been forced by the Nazi government to leave their families in Europe. Goldsmith's parents and their families lost nearly everything they owned, including their trust in people of authority.

Before the couple fled, the Nazis had restricted German-Jewish musicians such as Goldsmith's parents to an all-Jewish Culture Association (the Kulturbund or "Kubu"), which became their sole means of public performance. The music permitted by the Kubu was a source of solace to the couple. In this excerpt from Goldsmith's memoir, it is 1941 and Goldsmith's parents, Günther and Rosemarie Goldschmidt, are waiting at home in Berlin for the arrival of their tickets to the United States.

Every day he [Günther] and Rosemarie awaited the arrival of the mailman with intense suspense. When they had to be away and missed the daily delivery, they would always rush home in acute anticipation, telling themselves excitedly that today would be the day they would receive news about their passage to America. But days, weeks passed, and there was no word.

No word of rescue, that is. What did arrive occasionally were brief letters from Alex and Helmut [Günther's father and brother] from their captivity in Rivesaltes [a camp in France for enemy aliens] in which they described, in guarded words, their sufferings from exposure to rain and wind and an ever-present gnawing hunger that sapped their eroding reserves of strength and hope. Günther felt powerless to shape even his own fate, yet he was tormented by the conviction that he should somehow be

---

Martin Goldsmith, *The Inextinguishable Symphony*. New York: John Wiley & Sons, Inc., 2000. Copyright © 2000 by Martin Goldsmith. All rights reserved. Reproduced by permission of the publisher.

able to assist his father and brother. When he had wrestled with his troubled conscience for some time, usually at three or four in the morning, and concluded that there was really nothing he could do, he would resign himself to his helplessness with reassuring thoughts that at least Alex and Helmut were safe in France and far away from the dangers of living in Germany. What, after all, was the worst that could happen to them? With any luck at all they would simply ride out the war across the border, and after Hitler's inevitable defeat they would return home to the welcoming arms of their family.

In the face of such strains it was a great relief for Günther and Rosemarie to be able to concentrate on music. On April 3, the Kulturbund [Jewish cultural organization] Orchestra gave a concert that included the overture to the comic opera *The Bartered Bride* by Czech composer Bedřich Smetana and the *Serenade for Strings* by his compatriot Antonín Dvořák, as well as the Symphony in D Minor by the Belgian-born César Franck. The Dvořák and Franck pieces were new additions to my parents' repertory. Even though Günther's flute was not needed in the Dvořák, he characteristically studied the score and even attended a few rehearsals to heighten his understanding of the sometimes melancholy but largely cheerful *Serenade*.

This was the first concert mounted by the Kulturbund since the triumph of the *Resurrection* Symphony five weeks before. Kubu patrons had not seen a play since a production of a light comedy called *30-Second Love*, directed by Fritz Wisten, had opened on March 8. Diminished resources and dwindling energy combined to make each new endeavor an extreme test of the artists' wills. The more the Kulturbund cut back on its offerings, however, the more audiences seemed to appreciate them, and the concert on April 3 was another success, with a packed house and sustained ovations.

"We Have You Surrounded"

That evening, as the people ambled out of the theater into the early spring chill, they were confronted by an eerie and disquieting sight. A troop of Hitler Youth, both boys and girls, had assembled on the sidewalk, apparently for the express purpose of intimidation. Standing silently in neat rows and in full regalia, they stared fixedly at the older crowd of concertgoers, who averted their eyes and hurried off to arrive at their homes before curfew. The young people waited until all the patrons had left the building, then marched away, the last rays of the evening sun turning their blond heads golden.

The message was unmistakable: We have you surrounded and we may hurt you at any time. Even our children are your implacable enemies.

Three days later, on April 6, Palm Sunday, the German army continued its seemingly unstoppable advance, rolling into Greece and Yugoslavia. Excited announcers broadcast the news on German radio; one overwrought commentator likened the entry of German tanks into Athens to the humble entry of Jesus, astride a donkey, into Jerusalem two millennia ago.

The news of this latest victory inspired both organized and impromptu celebrations throughout the country. That night a phalanx of Brownshirts, augmented by a scattering of ordinary citizens, marched down Prinzenstrasse carrying flags and torches, singing Party songs and chanting paeans to their noble chancellor. Günther and Rosemarie gazed down onto the revelers from their window and then turned slowly to look at each other. They both sensed that time was running out for them; if they didn't secure passage on a ship soon, it would surely be too late.

Great News

And then, without warning, the longed-for, eagerly anticipated lightning bolt struck. On Thursday afternoon, April 10, in an unexceptional envelope, arrived two tickets for the Portuguese liner *Mouzhino*, scheduled to depart Lisbon for New York in precisely two months, on June 10.

My parents' wonder and disbelief and feelings of gratitude knew no bounds. Were they really going to escape the dangers that threatened them daily? They had secured a sponsor, passports, passage to the United States. But they celebrated quietly, secretly, not even telling their mothers the news for several days. They did not dare to believe wholeheartedly in their good fortune until they found themselves on U.S. soil. . . .

Günther and Rosemarie did their best during those weeks to keep their great news to themselves, letting on to none of their colleagues that their years in Germany were coming to a close. But after the concert on May 15 they confided in their conductor. Rudolf Schwarz was very sad at the prospect of losing them, yet overjoyed at their good fortune. He immediately offered to write them each a letter of recommendation, fully assuming that they would try to find orchestra jobs in America.

In letters dated May 19, 1941, Schwarz spoke highly of their musical talents. Of Günther he wrote, "He is a high-spirited musician with special technical and artistic abilities. His tone is warm, full and very beautiful, his clean intonation and technical brilliance are striking, and his musical intelligence enables him to be flexible enough to understand and support all the conductor's intentions. We have the confident expectation that Herr Goldschmidt, with the extraordinary diligence and artistic ambition he has exhibited up until now, will continue to develop into a wind player of the first rank."

Schwarz was even more complimentary when it came to Rosemarie. "We possess in her," he wrote, "a noted instrumentalist who both musically and technically is equal to the demands of the orchestral literature. Her playing is tonally and rhythmically flawless, representative of the finest aspects of stringed intrument style, and it is a great joy for the conductor to hear. We are losing in Frau Goldschmidt one of our most valuable members."

It seems as if my parents had made quite an impression on their boss. It does a son proud!

Travel Plans

The same Jewish relief organization that had secured their tickets on the *Mouzhino* also arranged for them to leave Berlin for Lisbon on Sunday morning, June 1. They would take a train via occupied Paris. Each was allowed to carry a single suitcase. The task of deciding what to take with them and what to leave behind was both agonizing and simple. Because they had very few objects of value aside from their instruments, most of what they chose were books and scores of music. On top of that, they brought a few favorite clothes and Julian's [Rosemarie's father's] little wooden fiddler. That was all.

A customs official visited their apartment to inspect each item. He made it very clear that no gold or silver could leave the country and then inspected each book and every piece of music to ensure that Günther and Rosemarie were not smuggling secret documents to the United States. Before leaving he informed them coldly that they could each take no more than four dollars out of Germany and that the rest of their small savings would be confiscated by the Reich. The official then asked for their passports, looked them over, and told Günther with more than a touch of glee in his voice that they were incomplete: he would have to visit the headquarters of the Gestapo to obtain a final stamp of approval.

A Chilling Encounter

The next morning was chilly and rainy. Günther walked about a mile from Prinzenstrasse to the gleaming new Gestapo [Nazi secret police] headquarters on Prince Albrechtstrasse. He stood outside for several minutes in the rain, working up the courage to enter. Once inside the building, he took a deep breath and stepped lightly across the white marble floor to a desk occupied by an officer with the death's head insignia of the SS emblazoned on his black uniform. Before Günther could speak, the officer did, at top volume: *"Verfluchtes Juden-Schwein! Mit Ihren nassen Dreckfüssen haben Sie ja nun den ganzen Boden verschmutzt!"* ("Cursed Jew-Pig! With your dirty wet feet you've soiled the whole floor!")

Günther turned pale and his heart stood still. Had he just forfeited his chance at freedom? Without a word, he reached into his pocket, slowly pulled out the passports, and as gently as he could laid them on the officer's desk. Not daring to meet the other's eyes, he gazed down at the "soiled" floor.

"So you want to leave the Fatherland, do you?" sneered the officer. "Well, good. Good riddance, I say, to you, to your little whore, and all the rest of your tribe."

With that, he reached into a drawer, pulled out a rubber stamp, and with four vicious motions of his right arm, as if he were grandly imagining his fist striking the face of one of his chosen victims instead of sitting at a desk with two documents and an ink pad, the Gestapo officer rendered my parents' passports legal.

He flung them at Günther, exclaiming, "Now get your dirty feet out of here!" Günther did not have to be told twice; he rushed out of the building and into the rain, deeply grateful that nothing truly bad had happened. But it was an incident that never left him; years later, he confessed that the image of that unknown man in uniform had always made it difficult for him to approach a policeman, even to ask for directions on an unfamiliar highway.

"The *Inextinguishable* Symphony"

And now, with only a few days remaining until their departure, came the last meeting with their colleagues in the Kulturbund. The 1940–1941 orchestral season was over, but [conductor] Rudolf Schwarz summoned his musicians for a final rehearsal, to read through the piece with which he intended to open the new season in the fall: the Symphony No. 4 by Danish composer Carl Nielsen.

Nielsen came from a musical household. His father, a housepainter by trade, played the violin at home and the cornet in his village band. Young Carl contributed to the family's income by herding geese, but he also found time to take piano lessons and learn fiddle playing from his father. At fourteen he became a regimental bugler in the 16th battalion of the Royal Danish Army. Five years later, in 1884, he entered the music conservatory in Copenhagen, beginning a career that produced some of the most fascinating and deeply felt music of his time.

The outbreak of World War I horrified him. "The whole world seems to be disintegrating," he wrote to a friend. "National feeling, which up to now was regarded as something lofty and beautiful, has instead become like a spiritual syphilis that has destroyed the brains, and it grins out through the empty eye sockets with moronic hate." Nielsen found his personal antidote to Europe's sickness in his deep belief in the power and beauty of music, which led him to begin work, in the fateful summer of 1914, on his Fourth Symphony.

[Nielsen] proclaimed that in his symphony he would "endeavor to indicate what music alone is capable of expressing to the full: the elemental will of life. In case all the world were to be devastated by fire, flood, and volcanoes, and all things were destroyed and dead, then nature would still begin to breed new life again. Soon the plants would begin to multiply again, the breeding and screaming of birds would be seen and heard, the aspiration and yearning of human beings would be felt."

"This," insisted the composer, "is music's own territory. Music *is* Life, and like Life, inextinguishable." From the day of its premiere, in 1916, Carl Nielsen's Fourth has been known as the *Inextinguishable* Symphony.

Life and Spirit

All this Rudolf Schwarz told his musicians when they gathered for a special rehearsal on a Thursday afternoon in late May of 1941.

"This is music," he said, "that speaks directly to our situation and that of our listeners. All of us—musicians, electricians, tailors, grocers, mothers, and fathers—need to be reminded that life is paramount. Even where it is stamped out, it eventually returns. Where there is life, there is spirit. And where there is spirit, where there is even one human soul, there is music. We are proof of that. We have suffered, yet we have endured. And we have made music."

Schwarz paused, cleared his throat and went on.

"And that is why I have asked you here this afternoon, to play through this symphony with me and to keep it in your hearts until we meet again to perform it for our public in the fall. Some of you, I know, will not be with us then. But wherever you are, a part of you will always be here. And you will have this music, this inextinguishable music, to remind you of us, always."

With that, Schwarz took up his baton and began the rehearsal.

The *Inextinguishable* Symphony begins aggressively, almost violently, as if reflecting the "syphilitic" condition of its origins. But less than two minutes in, a calm settles over the orchestra and the clarinets announce a sweet little melody that will recur several times throughout the next forty minutes. Nielsen describes a great struggle, suggesting the guns of war with a volley of blows hammered out by two sets of kettledrums on opposite sides of the stage. But through it all, the sweet melody persists, eventually taking on a defiant note of triumph in the symphony's final measures. It is a particularly moving and yet ambiguous triumph; the melody has a downward rather than an upward arc, as if Nielsen is emphasizing both the victory and the forces of destruction that must always be overcome.

Inspiration

Günther and Rosemarie had never heard or played music quite like this before. At the end they both had tears in their eyes, moved beyond words by the force of Nielsen's conviction and the success of his inspiration. Schwarz led the orchestra through the complete symphony once only, and then sat back while he and his musicians caught their breath.

"Thank you, ladies and gentlemen, for indulging my wishes. You see what an extraordinary piece this is. Go now, and have a lovely summer. We will see each other again in late September, when we will begin to work on this symphony in earnest. I believe that it will have a powerful effect on our audience."

Günther and Rosemarie slowly packed up their instruments and prepared to leave the theater for what they knew would be the last time. On their way to the street they knocked on Rudolf Schwarz's dressing room to say goodbye. He enveloped them both in a long embrace.

"How does that song go?" he asked Günther with a sad smile. "'Give my regards to Broadway?' Please, children," he continued softly, "be careful. And be happy. And remember us who are staying."

"How can we ever forget? Thank you," said Günther, "thank you a thousand times."

"For everything," added Rosemarie. "Including introducing us to that symphony today. As I was playing, I heard our story in its pages."

"Yes," said Schwarz. "It's the story of all of us, isn't it? 'Music is Life . . . ' Well, goodbye. I'm playing at the synagogue this weekend and have to run to another rehearsal."

Günther and Rosemarie took a long last look at the maze of corridors and dressing rooms that had been their home away from home for more than two and a half years. Then they trudged out into Kommandantenstrasse, the descending theme of Nielsen's Fourth sounding silently in their hearts.

Only hours remained of their lives in Germany. On Saturday night, May 31, they visited the little house on Manfred von Richthofenstrasse to say farewell to their mothers and Eva [Günther's sister]. It was chilly and rainy, and a mist of sorrow hung over the house. Adding to the gloom were the dim lights and shuttered windows mandated by the blackout. There were occasional lighthearted references to the day when the family would be reunited in America, and Toni [Günther's mother] reminded the children several times that they should do what they could to help the family once they arrived at their destination. But my father remembers his conviction that this would be the last time they would ever meet. He and Rosemarie had brought along a gift of fancy writing paper to ensure a steady stream of letters across the ocean, and everyone chattered gaily about how often they would write: three times a week, five times a week, every day! Toni presented the departing children with a precious memento: a dozen little silver-plated knives and forks, each of them only six inches long, that had belonged to her mother. Günther knew it was illegal to take this silverware out of Germany, but he was determined to smuggle it out anyway.

At last there seemed nothing more to say and Eva turned away to weep. Noticing his sister's tears, Günther stood up and declared, with mock severity "I have a new regulation to announce. Tonight, in bed, exactly ten minutes of sadness will be permitted under each blanket. But no more. After ten minutes, the household is ordered to consider only happy thoughts. Failure to comply with this edict will result in the most dire punishment. Am I completely understood?"

Toni and Else [Rosemarie's mother] nodded solemnly and Eva smiled and wiped her eyes.

After a long and weighty moment, everyone rose and walked out to the garden. Rain fell lightly into the enforced darkness. Drops of water coursed down the five faces as they exchanged their goodbyes. When my father hugged his mother for the last time, she whispered to him words that have never left him: *"Seid gut zu einander!"* ("Be good to each other!")

Holding each other by the hand, their eyes on the dark, damp ground Günther and Rosemarie walked slowly away. . . . Günther was painfully conscious of the irrevocable parting of the generations of his family.

A "Hole in My Heart"

Decades later, I recognize in this scene the source of the hole in my heart that nothing, not even the greatest happiness, has quite been able to fill. Within the garden gate stand three women, abandoned by husbands and father and now by children and brother, as a yet more horrible fate slouches towards them. Walking sadly away, like Adam and Eve banished from another garden, a burning guilt kindled within them, go my parents, embarking on a journey they would never have chosen in normal times. Trying hard not to think of either the past or the future, they steel themselves for the present, for an ordeal both frightening and liberating. And I, having never known anything but safety, can only contemplate their actions with awe.

At the appointed hour the next morning, Günther and Rosemarie reported to the Berlin Zoo railroad station with their suitcases and their instruments. Günther had wrapped his mother's miniature silverware in two pieces of soft cloth and hidden them in the lining of his pants. The organizers of the relief organization saw to it that all went like clockwork. The train cars were stifling and filled to capacity and their windows were painted black so that no one could see either in or out, but the locomotive pulled out of the station precisely on time. And how fortunate my parents were that they left Berlin on a train headed west instead of east!

Before reaching the French border, the train made brief stops in Merseburg, Erfurt, and Kaiserslautern, and each time Günther and Rosemarie stole a few moments to send a postcard back home to Richthofenstrasse. After a few hours Rosemarie managed to take a brief nap, but Günther stayed wide awake, kept from sleep by the hot, crowded conditions and by his own teeming excitement. Everything he saw seemed unreal, and several times he had to shake his head vigorously to reassure himself that he wasn't dreaming, that he really was on his way to freedom in America.

The passengers were not permitted to use the toilets on the train, but as it neared Paris the authorities announced that there would be a long rest stop. Everyone longed to catch a glimpse of the beautiful city; the paint on the windows, however, rendered that impossible. In the underground station, the passengers who wished to use the toilets were required to file through a double line of German soldiers stationed there to prevent anyone's attempting an escape into town—as if anyone wanted to! On their way back to the train, Günther paused for a moment to speak to Rosemarie and immediately one of the guards screamed at them to keep moving and to remain silent.

Regrets

As the train rolled west through occupied France, Günther's thoughts flew south, to his father and brother in their camp at Rivesaltes. How close they now seemed, and yet how much more in danger of falling into the clutches of the forces who held Paris! As he and Rosemarie approached their longed-for freedom, he was more conscious of the frightful vulnerability of his family.

At the border with Spain, Günther and Rosemarie saw German forces for the last time. They feared another encounter with [Nazi military and stormtrooper] SS or SA troops but were pleasantly surprised to find instead regular soldiers stationed at the border to check, once more, each item being taken out of the country. The young man who inspected their luggage stopped when he discovered their music and began to page through it.

Günther, fully conscious of the forbidden silverware he was hiding in his pants, summoned the courage to ask, "Do you read music?"

The soldier smiled. "Oh yes," he exclaimed eagerly. "Back home I played the organ in church. I hoped one day to study seriously, but . . ." He shrugged and hefted his rifle. "I play a different instrument now."

"And where is home?" Günther prodded, encouraged by the young man's manner.

"Leipzig," replied the soldier proudly. "Where Bach played for so many years."

"I hear it's a beautiful city," said Günther. He paused. "Now I suppose I'll never know."

"No, I suppose not." The young man stared at Günther for a moment. Then he placed the music carefully back into the suitcase, closed it, and handed it back.

"I'm sorry," he said softly. "Good luck to both of you."

"And to you, too," Günther and Rosemarie responded together. For years afterward, my father thought of the polite young soldier and wondered if he survived the war, and if he ever again played the organ in the city of Johann Sebastian Bach.

The Survival of Jazz Under Nazism

Michael Kater

During the 1920s, jazz and swing became sensations and typically were even more popular in Europe than in their native United States. Germany was no exception to this trend. Berlin enthusiastically welcomed American jazz artists, many of them African Americans. The dancer Josephine Baker, for one, found the city's nightclubs a dazzling haven. But the rise of the Nazi party during the 1930s turned this modern music into an underground art. Hitler and his propaganda minister Joseph Goebbels found jazz threatening because its creators were largely from two groups the Nazis despised—blacks and Jews. Also, because jazz was often improvised and embodied new rhythms, it clashed with the traditional, uniform German music the Nazis embraced.

The Nazi clampdown against jazz put some German enthusiasts in a bind. In the following excerpt, Michael Kater tells the story of Dietrich Schulz-Kohn, who found himself in a difficult position toward the end of World War II. This young military officer, as well as some other Germans, took considerable risks as they were squeezed between their positions in Germany, their love of jazz, and the approaching enemy armies. Kater is a history professor at York University in Toronto.

[In Berlin around 1943, jazz enthusiasts] Hans Blüthner and Gerd Peter Pick were trying to get by. Pick was in danger of being conscripted for forced labor . . . and to avert that, Blüthner attempted to offer him employment in his uncle's firm. That having failed, Pick found shelter in some other Berlin "war-conducive" business that looked after him acceptably, while his father, the Jew, was still in hiding in Berlin-Grunewald. How easy it would have been for the Gestapo to get the son to tell about it!

Michael Kater, *Different Drummers: Jazz in the Culture of Nazi Germany*. New York: Oxford University Press, 1992. Copyright © 1992 by Michael H. Kater. All rights reserved. Reproduced by permission of the publisher.

Blüthner himself courted disaster late in 1944 when he, too, was charged with having listened to the BBC for years. His uncle's business partner had been spying on him and had, in fact, goaded him on with constant questions about how the war was going. The Gestapo labeled the by now familiar charges against the young man: shirking active war service . . . consorting with foreigners, being beholden to jazz and, not least, being a friend of the Jews. In this context, Pick was specifically mentioned, and the secret police counted it against Hans that he had tried to help Pick out. However, since it was so late in the war and there was total confusion in the capital and absolutely no room for additional political prisoners, Blüthner luckily was let go by Christmas 1944.

It had escaped the Gestapo [secret police] that both Pick and Blüthner up to this time had been involved in a clandestine activity that could have brought them charges of high treason or defeatism. . . . In conjunction with Dietrich Schulz-Köhn, who irregularly dropped in from occupied France, they wrote, edited, and sent out a jazz newsletter. . . . they openly composed stories about condemned people and undesirables such as Jews (Artie Shaw and Benny Goodman), blacks (Benny Carter), and degenerate Frenchmen and Gypsies (Eddy Barclay and Django Reinhardt); they unashamedly lauded American jazz and its subculture; and, worst of all perhaps, they sent these full-featured "letters," four in all, to soldiers at the fronts and into neutral countries such as Sweden without any official authorization. . . .

Some of the news items were indeed hair-raising, because they were treated as classified information back in the Reich. One of these was the story that the black expatriate American trumpeter Harry Cooper had been performing somewhere in Paris just after having returned "fresh from the concentration camp, into which he had been clapped because he is an American." Even more incriminating was the fact that the half-Jew Pick, who would have had every reason to keep a low profile, had signed for at least one article (the story on Carter, with a clear-cut drawing of the black man). In a way, it was a continuation of the outlawed Berlin Magische Note [jazz] club, and hence, by extension, itself illegal. "We could have been hanged seven times," Hans Blüthner has mused in retrospect.

An Enigma

Schulz-Köhn and Blüthner agree that it was Schulz-Köhn, the Luftwaffe [air force] lieutenant, who provided the list of mostly military addressees and placed his own portrait, in full military regalia, on the cover of the first issue in late 1942, the latter intended as a protective shield, whatever good that may have done them. In any event, there is no doubt that despite his Wehrmacht [armed forces] status, or perhaps even because of it, Schulz-Köhn was assuming a considerable risk for his own person, because of the form in which the questionable content was presented, because of his collaboration with those two highly suspect Berliners, and because of the unauthorized mode of distribution.

As it happens, the example of Schulz-Köhn provides the final enigma in this history of jazz during the Third Reich. That may not be surprising after what the reader has learned about this highly individualistic activist on behalf of jazz in the period before the war. Until May 1945, Dietrich Schulz-Köhn remained the good German officer who had sworn his oath to the fatherland several years earlier, and at the same time, he virtually risked his life for jazz. He kept in close contact with [French jazz enthusiasts] Hugues Panassié and Charles Delaunay, the latter of whom after 1942 was deeply involved in the French resistance, using the Hot Club de France as a decoy. Undoubtedly, Dietrich knew this, and he helped him in efforts to republish, illegally, his 1938 *Discography*.

In late 1942, the Luftwaffe officer once again traveled to Paris to listen to his most favorite Gypsy guitarist, with whom he had his picture taken. . . . In this memorable photograph, Schulz-Köhn is flanked by the Gypsy and four colonial black musicians; at the very far left stands Henri Battut, a French Jew, who was actually in hiding and whom Dietrich was helping out with food stamps.

Still Promoting Jazz

In June 1943 Schulz-Köhn, dressed in his officer's uniform, also gave a radio lecture at Nîmes, in fluent French, in which he extolled the virtues and played the records of Django Reinhardt. In the Hot Club de Marseille, in Vichy France, the lieutenant spun the latest American discs that he had just received from Stockholm, in return for his collaboration as a correspondent for the Swedish tabloid *Orkester Journalen*.

And yet he also, around that time, traveled to Frankfurt on his way to Berlin or Magdeburg and met his friends, Jung, Bohländer, and now Charlie Petry. Until the early hours of the morning they had an argument in Hans Otto's student quarters during which the Frankfurters voiced their qualms, their doubts, their fears about the Third Reich and, in particular, what it was doing to jazz. Not to worry, retorted Schulz-Köhn, after the Final Victory jazz in Germany, and the entire Germanic realm, would become much stronger; it wasn't doing that badly right now. Although both Bohländer and Jung vouch for the contents of this conversation, Schulz-Köhn has not the slightest recollection of it; but neither does he deny that it actually took place.

Was this an attempt to square the circle once again? If one attaches mere thoughtlessness to the lieutenant's remarks about the future of jazz in Germany, then his involvement in the newsletter venture with Blüthner and Pick could be judged equally ingenuous; the political acumen disappears in both cases. Yet that might perhaps be too simple an equation. It is more likely that Schulz-Köhn was as serious about the newsletter business as a conscious activity with possible political consequences as he was about the future of a Nazi-ruled Germany. He was beguiled by Germany's military strength and his own role in it as an officer. It bolstered his personal authority, which had always been important to him. At the same time he felt deeply that jazz simply was not the evil the Nazis had made it out to be and that one might be able to convince them of this eventually. Hence a lot of clarification, of demonstration, was called for, even at some personal risk. And this was precisely what Schulz-Köhn was righteously engaged in, in Germany or France. Therefore a genuine jazz victim Schulz-Köhn was not (although he could have slipped up badly several times in the last remaining years), but neither was he on the persecuting side. To this day the enigma of the man remains impenetrable.

"Man, You Are a Cat!"

The end of Dietrich Schulz-Köhn's jazz and military careers in the Third Reich was nothing short of spectacular. His company had been locked in by Allied troops for months since the summer of 1944, at St. Nazaire on the Loire River, near Rennes. There were captured Frenchmen, some wounded, held by the German troops in that pocket. An attempt to negotiate their release through the International Red Cross was made several times, the last one early in 1945. Schulz-Köhn, fluent in both French and English, was chosen by the German side to meet the Allies as its representative. Under the protection of a white flag, he approached the American officer in the enemy camp. The American looked at the Nazi lieutenant's Rolleiflex camera, slung about the Wehrmacht leather coat. He wanted to have this camera and offered to exchange it for Lucky Strikes cigarettes. Schulz-Köhn declined, saying that he happened to be interested in jazz records. His counterpart's offer to give him recordings by the Budapest String Quartet or Leopold Stokowski resulted in the following exchange, recounted later by Schulz-Köhn. "'No, I would like to know what Count Basie, Benny Goodman, and Lionel Hampton sound like right now.' He was flabbergasted. He looked at me and said: 'Have you ever heard of Panassié? You know Delaunay?' I said: 'Man, you are a cat!'" With this the ice was broken, an armistice was soon arranged, and prisoners from both sides were exchanged. The story surfaced in various American media, including the U.S. Army's *Stars and Stripes* [newspaper], in which Schulz-Köhn, in March 1945, was introduced, somewhat unkindly, as "tall, bespectacled Oberleutnant Schulz-Kroehn [*sic*], a high-voiced nervous Jazz fan from Berlin, whose passion is hot records."

On 8 May 1945, the day of the Third Reich's capitulation, Lieutenant First-Class Dr. Dietrich Schulz-Köhn was taken prisoner by the Americans. In the POW camp it was Hugues Panassié and Charles Delaunay from whom he received morale-boosting letters and care packages. Both men had inspired the German jazz fan decisively nearly fifteen years earlier. Jazz had conquered.

Mobilizing Germans for Economic Victory

Nicholas Levis

During the 1930s, the Nazis jump-started the depressed German economy by way of speeches and orchestrated events promoting a road-building and automobile-manfacturing program. This manufactured enthusiasm for building sleek highways and a "car of the people" was then quietly channeled into military production that enabled Germany to begin World War II. Government-mandated membership in a docile labor union that held staged pep rallies was the next step in building the nation's military capabilities. As armament production surged, the German people benefited from plundered wealth and were led to support Nazi goals with promises of new lands. Car buyers were even enticed via propaganda into a pay-now-buy-later scheme for Volkswagens they did not receive.

The following excerpt by American writer Nicholas Levis is from a study that reveals that American companies were involved in Germany's economic build-up. He shows how the Nazis combined vigorous information manipulation, economic maneuvers, and strong-arm control to achieve military domination.

Hitler's first major public speech as head of state was delivered on 10 February 1933, at the Berlin sports stadium. Playing on religious overtones, he brought the crowd into a tumult: "German people, give us four years time, then judge us."

The next day, Hitler spoke at the opening ceremonies of the Berlin "AA" motor show. There he announced a huge road-building program. Based on Weimar-era plans that had gone unfulfilled, this was to become the Nazis' largest non-military public spending item. Hitler lifted the tax on new car purchases, and promised that the motor industry would henceforth be organized as a key sector separate from the rest of the transport system.

Nicholas Levis, "Prologue," in *Working for the Enemy: Ford, General Motors, and Forced Labor in Germany During the Second World War*, by Reinhold Billstein, Karola Fings, Anita Kugler, and Nicholas Levis, edited by Nicholas Levis. New York: Berghahn Books, 2000. Copyright © 2000 by Nicholas Levis. All rights reserved. Reproduced by permission of the publisher.

At the next Berlin motor show, in March 1934, he revealed plans to create a *Volkswagen*—a car of the people that would sell for under 1,000 reichsmarks, and thus be affordable to most households. This idea captured the imagination of a great number of the German people. Construction of the first *Autobahn* began that month, with Hitler briefly digging the turf as thousands cheered. The state hired hundreds of thousands of workers for its mobile construction squads. Starting in 1935, the Autobahns "linked Germany from border to border and were the first integrated network of express highways in the world." They "became a model for all future highway construction," as the automotive historian James Flink writes.

Volksmotorisierung was the original centerpiece of Nazi economic policy. The military build-up was started in secret, so as not to antagonize the still-dominant Western powers, but "popular motorization" could be pursued with a maximum of fanfare. That motorization also had a military effect, whatever the intent, is clear. The products of the German auto industry would prove vital in powering the Blitzkrieg. The Autobahn was of secondary importance. Incapable of bearing heavy armor, during the war it was useful for shuttling supplies among German arms plants. Otherwise, *Motorisierung* tremendously increased demand in the materials processing and supply industries, and stimulated their development. Three thousand kilometers of new road were completed and over three thousand bridges built by 1939.

Economic Salvation

Quite beyond the direct increase in demand, these powerful and early signals encouraged the auto industry to invest and expand. The carmakers of Germany, at first uncertain about the Nazis' announced commitment to their industry, were quickly won over by the results. Overall production of vehicles increased from about 52,000 in 1932 to 342,000 in 1938. By that time the motor sector employed 1.5 million people, representing one out of every twelve jobs. The consumer market had expanded insofar as the country's gross national product more than doubled, to 130 billion RM [Reichmarks, the German currency until 1948] in 1939, and unemployment was wiped out. Starting already in 1934–1935, however, the emphasis in Nazi policy had turned decisively away from the mass market, and towards armaments. German car production in the late 1930s was still much less than a tenth of U.S. production in 1927.

As the largest German carmaker, and as a maker of small cars, Opel [owned by the huge American firm General Motors] was a primary and early beneficiary of German motorization. Compared to a 1929–1933 average of about 24,000 units, domestic sales of Opel cars more than tripled by 1938, to 85,497 units. . . . In the same period General Motors doubled its plant investment, raising employment at Russelsheim to about 20,000 people. . . .

From Private Cars to Military Vehicles

By late 1934 the Nazis had consolidated their total control over all aspects of German politics and society. Regional parliaments were dissolved in January 1934. Hitler Youth was made into a compulsory state organization. . . .

All members of the armed forces were compelled to swear loyalty directly to the Führer in August. A rigged referendum to

Hitler is sworn in as chancellor on January 30, 1933.

give Hitler unconditional powers received a 90 percent "yes" vote on 19 August. That was the last official election result under 99 percent. . . .

Already in 1934, the Reich's spending on the military far exceeded spending on transport, and after 1935 spending on all other programs combined. Opel entered the booming arms business in 1935. At the behest of the armed forces, the company agreed to build a new truck plant in Brandenburg, south of Berlin. The Wehrmacht believed that only Opel had the resources and expertise to build such a large factory in the shortest possible time. . . . In January 1936, the largest and most efficient truck plant in Europe began producing the Opel Blitz, a line of light and medium-weight trucks usable as troop and supply carriers. Unit production rose from about 14,000 in the first year to more than 24,000 in 1939. After the annexation of the Czech Sudetenland in October 1938, the Opel Blitz was sold almost exclusively to the German armed forces.

Opel's Russelsheim factory had a pre-1933 history of strong, Social Democratic unionism as well as periods of effective Communist organizing. It was the scene of various clandestine activities after 1933, although most of the underground was smashed by the Gestapo in a nationwide crackdown on resistance groups in 1935. The handful of groups who remained met in small, paranoid cells. A company network of informants reported daily to the Gestapo and the management. In the coach department, a brief strike was staged in June 1936, protesting low wages and poor conditions. All of the workers in the department were fired on the spot. Many of them were arrested. A few ended up in the camps. Any kind of labor action was by then exceedingly rare. Even years later, the more committed Nazis among the authorities regarded Opel (and the Americans involved in its management, who were often said to be under "Jewish influence") with suspicion. . . .

The War Machine

In 1936, as they showed their best face to the world in preparation for the Berlin Olympics of August, the Nazis embarked upon increasingly obvious preparations for war. In its first open intervention abroad, the Reich dispatched its Legion Condor to fight on behalf of Franco and the fascists in the Spanish civil war. Berlin's expenditures on the Wehrmacht [armed forces] alone shot from 5.1 billion RM in 1935 up to 9.0 billion RM in 1936 (by 1939: 16.5 billion RM). . . .

In place of the mass market initially hoped for by many businessmen, the Nazis had created an economy in which the state, as the buyer of armaments and military supplies, was the top customer of private corporations. Acknowledging the rights of private ownership, as long as it was "Aryan," the Reich still kept a firm rein on wages and hence on popular buying power. The armaments program became an economic stimulant from which Germany, if it was not to fall back into economic crisis, could never afford to back down. . . .

"Strength Through Joy"

With their businesses nonetheless booming by comparison to the crisis years, auto industry executives were . . . interested in neutralizing the Volkswagen project, which had run into financial difficulties. The industrialists secretly hoped the Volkswagen would be produced by a state concern, and also feared exactly that. Finally, in the spring of 1937, Hitler designated the KdF ("Strength through Joy") department of DAF [the only legal labor organization] as his desired carrier for the Volkswagen project.

Strength through Joy was the DAF branch charged with organizing recreation and travel for workers. The DAF had turned into the largest mass organization of the Nazi Party. It counted twenty-one million members in 1939, and assured a docile workforce, which in Nazi jargon was called "the Following" (*Gefolgschaft*). Company managers were referred to as "leaders" (*Betriebsführer*). At each workplace a political "Shopfloor Leader" (*Betriebsobmann*) was appointed especially by the party. An archaic "leadership principle" was enshrined in company organization.

At Opel, as at other workplaces, the personnel were gathered about once a month at compulsory rallies, where hours of propaganda speeches were delivered by company and party officials. To get a job, a worker had to present his or her *Arbeitsbuch*. This booklet documented employment history as recorded by the employer and the authorities. The *Arbeitsbuch* was one of many means used to tie workers to their jobs in a tight labor market, although in practice companies tended to hire workers even against the rules.

After DAF took over the Volkswagen project, Porsche and DAF ignored the existing auto industry and created an independent, state-owned Volkswagen plant. . . . The company later known as Volkswagenwerk GmbH was founded in May 1937. "The building of the Volkswagenwerk was carried out according to American models and aimed at applying the most advanced techniques used at Ford plants in Detroit.". . .

Aggression, Persecution, and Deception

The real focus of the Reich's foreign policy remained on *Lebensraum*—ample "living-space" for the supposedly overcrowded German people, as called for in *Mein Kampf*. That meant central and eastern Europe, starting with Austria and Czechoslovakia, but going on to Poland and the territories of "the East.". . . In November 1937 Hitler ordered the Wehrmacht to plan for total war.

The next year accordingly began with renewed threats against Germany's neighbors. . . .

On 9 November 1938, after the shooting of a German consul abroad, the Nazis orchestrated a nationwide pogrom against the German Jews. Hundreds were killed, synagogues burned to the ground. . . . The total exclusion of Jews from social and economic life was now completed. All Jewish property, which the Nazis had ordered registered in April, was expropriated and given over to "pure" German owners, a process known as "Aryanization." This had in reality begun years before, as banks refused to extend credits to Jewish-owned businesses, forcing the owners to sell at below-market prices.

A few months later, in March 1939, with its agents stirring up further unrest in Czechoslovakia, the Reich occupied the rest of that now defenseless country. . . .

The huge Volkswagen plant, the "German River Rouge," was nearing completion in Lower Saxony. The factory and the new city nearby were supposed to serve as models of Nazi industriousness and German superiority. A VW auxiliary plant, set up in Braunschweig, trained an elite of German production workers in a basically military regime. This was appropriate, as most of them would end up on the front, not the assembly line. The factory would soon produce warplane parts and the Wehrmacht's trademark "bucket cars," based on Porsche's design. The majority of the workforce would be forced laborers.

Hitler had announced that the Volkswagen was to be called the "KdFCar." The new town became known as the "City of the KdF Car" (which it was called until the British renamed it Wolfsburg in 1945). The DAF's propaganda offensives trumpeted the "KdF" savings scheme as the means for workers to purchase the cars that the Volkswagen plant would one day produce: "5 Marks a Week to Save—If You Want to Drive Your Own Car!" As the number of people in the concentration camps and prisons swelled to 300,000 by April 1939, millions of Germans dreamed of owning a KdF Car.

Only the Volkswagenwerk management knew that its price would have to be at least twice what was being advertised. Intended to finance production once the plant was completed, the savings scheme was a swindle. The 280 million RM gathered from the 336,000 subscribers served as the fodder for corrupt dealings within the DAF. Even after the war started, with the VW plant switching to military production and refusing car orders, the propaganda encouraged front soldiers to keep paying into the scheme. Production start of the KdF Car was originally scheduled for late summer 1939.

Chronology

1889
Adolf Hitler is born in Austria.

1914–1918
World War I; Hitler serves as a corporal in the German army.

November 11, 1918
Germany signs the armistice ending World War I.

January 2, 1919
The German Workers' Party is founded in Munich by Karl Harrer and Anton Drexler.

February 1919
A new democratic German constitution is drafted in Weimar and Germany becomes known as the Weimar Republic.

June 28, 1919
The Treaty of Versailles is signed, imposing harsh punishments on Germany.

September 16, 1919
Hitler becomes a member of the German Workers' Party.

February 24, 1920
Hitler makes a speech in Munich presenting the party's twenty-five-point program.

March 1920
The German Workers' Party changes its name to the National Socialist German Workers' Party, or Nazi Party.

1921
Hitler asserts himself as the unchallenged leader of the Nazis and establishes the *Sturmabteilung* (SA).

January 1923
French forces occupy the Ruhr after Germany defaults on reparations payments.

May 1923
Julius Streicher begins publishing the anti-Semitic newspaper *Der Stürmer*.

November 1923
Hitler and his followers attempt a revolution, or putsch, at a Munich beer hall; the coup fails, the Nazi Party is banned, and Hitler is arrested.

February 24, 1924
Hitler and other Nazis stand trial for treason, after which Hitler is sentenced to five years in prison.

April 1–December 20, 1924
Hitler serves his sentence in Landsberg Prison; he begins to write *Mein Kampf*.

May 4, 1924
Former Nazi members, running in other parties, are elected to the German Reichstag.

February 1925
Hitler revives the Nazi Party, convincing authorities to lift its ban after promising to stage no more military coups.

April 26, 1925
Former field marshal Paul von Hindenburg is elected president of Germany.

June 1925
The *Schutzstaffel* (SS) is formed.

July 1925
The first volume of *Mein Kampf* is published.

August 19, 1927
The Nazi Party holds its first rally in Nuremberg.

May 1928
Nazis receive 2.6 percent of the vote in national elections; twelve Nazi members are elected to the Reichstag.

November 1928
Joseph Goebbels takes over the propaganda activities of the Nazi Party.

January 6, 1929
Heinrich Himmler is made head of the SS, which is set to be established as Hitler's bodyguard.

October 29, 1929
The U.S. stock market crashes, setting off a worldwide economic depression that greatly affects Germany for several years.

September 1930
Nazis gain 18 percent of the vote and 107 Reichstag seats in the national elections.

March 13, 1932
Hitler finishes second to Hindenburg in the presidential election; Hindenburg wins a subsequent runoff.

July 31, 1932
Nazis win 230 seats and become the strongest party in the Reichstag.

January 30, 1933
Hindenburg appoints Hitler to be chancellor.

February 1933
Fire destroys the Reichstag building; Hitler blames Communists and is given emergency governing powers by Hindenburg.

March 13, 1933
Goebbels is made minister for public enlightenment and propaganda.

March 23, 1933
The Reichstag passes the Enabling Act, giving Hitler dictatorial powers.

April 1933
Nazis promote a national boycott of Jewish businesses and later pass their first anti-Jewish laws.

May 1933
German Labor Front (DAF) is established as the only legal and compulsory labor union.

May 10, 1933
Book-burning campaigns throughout Germany destroy books by Jewish and liberal authors.

July 14, 1933
All political parties besides the Nazi Party are banned in Germany.

October 14, 1933
Germany withdraws from an international disarmament conference and the League of Nations.

June 30, 1934
Hitler orders the arrest and execution of opponents within the Nazi Party in what becomes known as the Night of Long Knives.

August 2, 1934
President Hindenburg dies; Hitler combines the offices of president and chancellor to become the führer of Germany.

March 6, 1935
The first issue of *Das Schwarze Korps*, the newspaper of the SS, is issued.

March 16, 1935
Hitler announces the formation of the military draft and the creation of a German air force (the Luftwaffe), both in violation of the Treaty of Versailles.

September 15, 1935
The Nuremberg Laws are passed, stripping Jews of citizenship rights, forbidding Jews to marry non-Jews, and barring Jews from many professions.

March 7, 1936
German troops occupy the demilitarized Rhineland.

June 17, 1936
Himmler is appointed chief of secret police.

Summer 1936
The Olympic Games are held in Berlin.

January 30, 1937
Hitler declares the Treaty of Versailles to be void.

March 1938
Germany annexes Austria.

September 1938
Britain and France attempt to appease Hitler by giving Germany the Sudetenland, a part of Czechoslovakia.

November 9–10, 1938
Nazis incite a violent rampage against Jewish shops and synagogues in *Kristallnacht* (Night of the Broken Glass).

March 1939
Germany occupies the rest of Czechoslovakia.

August 23, 1939
Germany and the Soviet Union sign a nonaggression pact.

September 1, 1939
Germany invades Poland.

September 3, 1939
France and Britain declare war on Germany, beginning World War II.

May 10, 1940
Germany attacks France, Belgium, the Netherlands, and Luxembourg.

June 21, 1940
France surrenders to Nazi Germany.

August 13, 1940
The Battle of Britain begins as Germany launches an air attack.

September 27, 1940
Germany, Italy, and Japan agree to assist one another by signing the Tripartite Pact.

June 22, 1941
Germany invades the Soviet Union.

August 1941
Nazis stop all Jewish emigration from Germany and introduce the requirement for Jews to wear yellow stars in public.

December 1941
The first German death camp opens in Chelmno, Poland.

December 7, 1941
Japan bombs Pearl Harbor; America enters the war against Japan.

December 11, 1941
Hitler declares war on the United States.

December 16, 1941
Hitler assumes personal command of the German armed forces.

1942
Tide of war turns against Germany in North Africa; British and U.S. planes begin massive terror bombing of German cities.

January 20, 1942
Nazi leaders at the Wannsee Conference draw up plans for the Final Solution—the genocide of the Jews.

November 1942
The German Sixth Army besieging Stalingrad is surrounded by Soviet troops.

January 27, 1943
The United States launches its first bombing attacks on Germany.

January 31–February 2, 1943
German soldiers surrender to the Soviets in Stalingrad in opposition to Hitler's orders.

June 6, 1944
Allied troops land on the Normandy coast of France.

July 20, 1944
Hitler survives an assassination attempt by German military personnel.

April 20, 1945
Hitler makes his last public appearance.

April 30, 1945
Hitler commits suicide in his Berlin bunker.

May 7, 1945
Admiral Karl Dönitz arranges for Germany's unconditional surrender to the Allies.

November 20, 1945
Top Nazi officials go on trial at Nuremberg.

October 16, 1946
Nine leading Nazis are convicted and executed at Nuremberg.

For Further Research

William Sheridan Allen, *The Nazi Seizure of Power: The Experience of a Single German Town, 1930–1935*. New York: New Viewpoints, 1973.

Werner T. Angress, *Between Fear and Hope: Jewish Youth in the Third Reich*. New York: Columbia University Press, 1988.

Raymond Aron, *Democracy and Totalitarianism*. Ann Arbor: University of Michigan Press, 1994.

Eugene Aroneanu, comp., *Inside the Concentration Camps: Eyewitness Accounts of Life in Hitler's Death Camps*. Trans. Thomas Whissen. Westport, CT: Praeger, 1996.

Norman H. Baynes, ed., *The Speeches of Adolf Hitler, April 1922–August 1939*. 2 vols. New York: Howard Fertig, 1969.

Doris L. Bergen, *Twisted Cross: The German Christian Movement in the Third Reich*. Chapel Hill: University of North Carolina Press, 1996.

Reinhold Billstein et al., *Working for the Enemy: Ford, General Motors, and Forced Labor in Germany During the Second World War*. New York: Berghahn Books, 2000.

Fritz Brennecke and Nationalsozialistische Deutsche Arbeiter-Partei, *Hitlerjugend: The Nazi Primer Official Handbook for Schooling the Hitler Youth*. New York: Harper, 1938.

Michael Burleigh, *Death and Deliverance: "Euthanasia" in Germany c. 1900–1945*. New York: Cambridge University Press, 1994.

———, *The Third Reich: A New History*. New York: Hill and Wang, 2000.

Joan Campbell, *Joy in Work, German Work: The National Debate, 1800–1945*. Princeton, NJ: Princeton University Press, 1989.

Gustavo Corni, *Hitler and the Peasants: Agrarian Policy of the Third Reich, 1930–1939*. New York: Berg, 1990.

Gordon A. Craig, *Germany, 1866–1945*. Oxford, UK: Oxford University Press, 1978.

Geoff Eley, ed., *Society, Culture, and the State in Germany, 1870–1930*. Ann Arbor: University of Michigan Press, 1998.

Joachim Fest, *Hitler*. Trans. Richard and Clara Winston. New York: Harcourt Brace Jovanovich, 1974.

———, *Speer: The Final Verdict*. New York: Harcourt, 1999.

Klaus P. Fischer, *Nazi Germany: A New History*. New York: Continuum, 1995.

Saul Friedlander, *Nazi Germany and the Jews: The Years of Persecution, 1933–1939*. London: Weidenfeld & Nicholson, 1998.

Carl J. Friedrich and Zbigniew K. Brzezinski, *Totalitarian Dictatorship and Autocracy*. 2nd ed. Cambridge, MA: Harvard University Press, 1965.

Peter Gay, *Freud, Jews, and Other Germans: Masters and Victims in Modernist Culture*. New York: Oxford University Press, 1978.

Robert Gellately, *Backing Hitler: Consent and Coercion in Nazi Germany*. Oxford, UK: Oxford University Press, 2001.

Daniel Jonah Goldhagen, *Hitler's Willing Executioners: Ordinary Germans and the Holocaust*. New York: Alfred A. Knopf, 1996.

Richard Grunberger, *A Social History of the Third Reich*. London: Weidenfeld & Nicholson, 1971.

———, *The 12-Year Reich: A Social History of Nazi Germany, 1933–1945*. New York: Holt, Rinehart, and Winston, 1971.

Alfons Heck, *The Burden of Hitler's Legacy*. Frederick, CO: Renaissance House, 1988.

Adolf Hitler, *Adolf Hitler: My New Order*. Ed. Raoul de Roussy de Sales. New York: Reynal & Hitchcock, 1941.

———, *Mein Kampf*. Trans. Ralph Manheim. Boston: Houghton Mifflin, 1971.

Harold James, *A Germany Identity, 1770–1990*. London: Routledge, 1989.

Ian Kershaw, *Hitler, 1889–1936: Hubris*. London: Penguin Books, 2001.

———, *Hitler, 1937–1945: Nemesis*. London: Penguin Books, 2001.

———, *The "Hitler Myth": Image and Reality in the Third Reich*. Oxford, UK: Oxford University Press, 1987.

Victor Klemperer, *I Shall Bear Witness: The Diaries of Victor Klemperer*. London: Weidenfeld & Nicholson, 1998.

Eugene Kogon, *The Theory and Practice of Hell.* Trans. Heinz Norden. New York: Berkley Books, 1998.

Peter Matheson, *The Third Reich and the Christian Churches.* Grand Rapids, MI: W.B. Eerdmans, 1981.

Bronwyn Rebekah McFarland-Icke, *Nurses in Nazi Germany: Moral Choice in History.* Princeton, NJ: Princeton University Press, 1999.

Wolfgang J. Mommsen, *Imperial Germany, 1867–1918: Politics, Culture, and Society in an Authoritarian State.* London: Hodder Arnold, 1995.

George L. Mosse, *Nazi Culture: Intellectual, Cultural, and Social Life in the Third Reich.* New York: Grosset & Dunlop, 1966.

Ingo Muller, *Hitler's Justice: The Courts of the Third Reich.* Cambridge, MA: Harvard University Press, 1991.

Klaus-Jurgen Muller, *The Army, Politics, and Society in Germany, 1933–45: Studies in the Army's Relation to Nazism.* Manchester, UK: Manchester University Press, 1987.

Benno Muller-Hill, *Murderous Science: Elimination by Scientific Selection of Jews, Gypsies, and Others, Germany, 1933–1945.* Oxford, UK: Oxford University Press, 1988.

Jeremy Noakes and Geoffrey Pridham, eds., *Nazism, 1919–1945: A Documentary Reader.* 4 vols. Exeter, UK: University of Exeter Press, 1983–1988.

Peter Novick, *The Holocaust in American Life.* Boston: Houghton Mifflin, 1999.

Robert J. O'Neill, *The German Army and the Nazi Party, 1933–1939.* London: Cassell, 1966.

Alison Owings, *"Frauen," German Women Recall the Third Reich.* New Brunswick, NJ: Rutgers University Press, 1993.

Jonathan Petropoulos, *The Faustian Bargain: The Art World in Nazi Germany.* New York: Oxford University Press, 2000.

Robert Proctor, *Racial Hygiene: Medicine Under the Nazis.* Cambridge, MA: Harvard University Press, 1988.

Peter G. Pulzer, *Germany, 1870–1945: Politics, State Formation, and War.* Oxford, UK: Oxford University Press, 1997.

Ralf Georg Reuth, *Goebbels.* New York: Harcourt Brace, 1990.

Gitta Sereny, *The Healing Wound: Experiences and Reflections on Germany, 1938–2001*. New York: W.W. Norton, 2001.

———, *Into That Darkness: From Mercy Killing to Mass Murder*. New York: McGraw-Hill, 1974.

William L. Shirer, *This Is Berlin*. New York: Overlook, Peter Mayer, 1999.

Albert Speer, *Inside the Third Reich: Memoirs by Albert Speer*. Trans. Richard and Clara Winston. New York: Macmillan, 1970.

Norman Stone, *Hitler*. London: Little, Brown, 1980.

Websites

German History, www.csustan.edu/History/faculty/Weikart/gerhist.htm. This site is maintained by Professor Richard Weikart and contains numerous links that relate to the Nazi period.

Nazi Germany and the Rise of Hitler, www.bbc.co.uk/education/modern/hitler/hitlehtm.htm and www.bbc.co.uk/education/modern/nazi/nazihtm.htm. This website is maintained by the British Broadcasting Corporation and contains information and photos about Adolf Hitler, the economy of Nazi Germany, and more.

The Origins, Nature, and Consequences of National Socialism, http://homes.jcu.edu.au/~hipgt/nazism/index.html. This website is maintained by Professor Paul Turnbull and contains information and links on such subjects as Adolf Hitler, Nazi racial policies, and the Nazi seizure of power.

Index

Aktion program, 12
art, 17, 22, 100
Aryan race, 17, 40, 43
  breeding of, 73
  description of, 13, 15, 20, 45
Auschwitz, 14, 32
Autobahn system, 10, 13, 135–36

Barclay, Eddy, 131
Bar-On, Dan, 76–77
Battut, Henri, 132
Bauhaus school, 11
Berliner, Emile, 10
Best, Werner, 29–31
blacks, Nazi treatment of, 40–47, 130–32
Blüthner, Hans, 130–33
Bormann, Martin (elder), 58, 61, 62, 75, 78–80, 83–84
Bormann, Martin (younger), 75, 78–84
Bosselman, Ursula, 48–53
Braun, Eva, 17, 57, 58–62, 75
Brendler, Konrad, 77–78
Buchenwald, 32–39

Carter, Benny, 131
Catholics, in German society, 85, 88, 90, 92–93, 95
censorship
  book burning as, 117
  of films, 108
  of newspapers, 12, 106, 112, 131
  of photos, 106
  of radio broadcasts, 86, 101, 131
Chamberlain, Neville, 111
children
  education of, 13, 40–47, 79–80, 89–91

Hitler and, 61, 62, 75, 79
of Nazis, 72–84, 87
Churchill, Winston, 104, 105
Communists, 14, 20, 23, 24, 41, 85, 89, 105–109
concentration camps
  criminals in, 24, 101
  despised people in, 20–21
  escape from, 35–36
  expansion of, 28, 29, 141
  in France, 119–20
  Jews in, 14, 15, 32, 37, 48, 66–68, 80
  life in, 32–39
  music in, 37–38
  propaganda about, 101
  SS in, 34–35, 80
Cooper, Harry, 131
Crane, Cynthia, 48
Czechoslovakia, 140

Dachau, 80, 83
DAF, 139–41
death camps. *See* concentration camps
Delaunay, Charles, 132, 134
Deutsche Werkbund (German Association of Craftsmen), 10–11
Domagk, Gerhard, 9

Einsatzgruppen (Special Action Groups), 74
eugenics, 11–12
euthanasia, 12, 20, 73

Fascists, 29–31, 139
film, Nazis use of, 41, 100–101, 104–12
Final Solution, 74

154

Fischer, Klaus, 9, 12–13
Flink, James, 136
Ford Motor Company, 10, 13, 137
Frank, Hans, 31
Führer-Leibstandarte (Hitler's guard), 81

Gellately, Robert, 22
General Motors, 10, 137
genocide, 9, 11, 14–15, 74, 91
George, Heinrich, 41
Germany
  automobile production in, 10, 13, 136–41
  class structure of, 10
  communication in, 9–10
  crime in, 14, 20, 22–31, 101
  culture of, 8
  depression in, 10, 13, 22, 24, 55–56, 86, 135
  economy of, 10–11, 56, 135–41
  guilt feelings and, 77–78
  invasion of Greece by, 121
  invasion of Yugoslavia by, 121
  police system of, 20–21, 22–31, 56
  as totalitarian state, 9
  transportation in, 10, 13, 135–41
  workers in, 135–41
Gerung, Pan, 64
Gestapo (secret police)
  as above the law, 28–31
  Goebbels and, 104
  head of, 73, 74
  headquarters of, 123
  interrogation and, 88, 130
  mission of, 30
  protective custody by, 24, 29
  smashes union, 138
Goebbels, Joseph, 40, 100, 103, 117, 130

Goldschmidt, Günther, 119–28
Goldschmidt, Rosemarie, 119–28
Goldsmith, Martin, 119
Goodman, Benny, 131, 134
Göring, Hermann, 60, 110
Great Britain, and war against Germany, 103–109
Gypsies, 14–15, 20, 32

Hampton, Lionel, 134
Heck, Alfons, 85
Hertz, Heinrich, 9
Heydrich, Reinhard, 74, 103
Heydrich, Thomas, 74
Himmler, Heinrich, 28–29, 31, 78, 83, 111
Hindenburg, Paul von, 27, 89
Hippler, Fritz, 104, 106
Hitler, Adolf
  assassination attempt on, 110–12
  becomes chancellor, 20, 22, 89
  everyday life of, 57–62, 84
  hatred of Jews and, 15, 20, 93, 104, 108, 116, 118
  on legal system, 27
  personality of, 8, 11, 55–56, 97–98
  popular support for, 15, 56, 86–87, 98, 109
  racial prejudices of, 20, 28, 56
  radio broadcasts by, 12, 85–86, 113
  suicide of, 75, 80
Hitlerjugend (Hitler Youth movement),
  activities of, 13, 42, 44, 94, 96, 120–21
  as compulsory, 13, 137
  forbidden to join, 40–47, 52, 92
  indoctrination of, 13, 40–41, 50, 88–90, 104

recruitment for, 13, 40–47, 97–98
uniform of, 44, 96–97
Hitlerjunge Quecks (film), 41
homosexuals, 14, 22, 32
Hot Club de Marseille, 132

Isherwood, Christopher, 23

Jews
  in German society, 14–15, 90–94, 140
  laws against, 28, 43, 48–53, 56, 90, 92
  leaving Germany of, 119–29
  Ostjuden and, 92
  pogroms against, 74, 140
  propaganda against, 90, 101–102, 104, 106, 108–109, 117
  relief organization for, 122
  restrictions on, 119–29
Jungmädel (Young Girls), 13
Jungvolk (Young Germans), 13, 41–47, 89, 96

Kapos (Jewish police), 80
Kater, Michael, 130
Kerbo, Harold R., 8
Koehn, Ilse, 16–17
Kogon, Eugene, 32
Kripo (criminal police), 24
Kristallnacht (Night of the Broken Glass), 74, 77
Kulturbund (Jewish Culture Association), 119, 120, 124

labor organizations, 135, 138, 139
Lammers, Hans, 110
Lebensborn, 73
Lebensraum, 140
Legacy of Silence (Bar-On), 76
Levis, Nicholas, 135

Lloyd George, David, 103

Massaquoi, Hans, 40
medicine, 8, 9, 11–12
Mein Kampf (Hitler), 20, 83, 140
Molotov, Vyacheslav, 107
Moser, Baurath, 63, 67
music
  classical, 119–29
  in concentration camps, 37–38
  in Germany, 10, 22, 130
  jazz, 130–34
  restrictions on, 119–29, 130–34
  use of, by Nazis, 12–13, 86, 107, 130

National Socialism, 9, 30–31, 79, 98, 113–18
Nationalsozialistische Deutsche Arbeiterpartei (NSADP, National Socialist German Workers' Party). *See* Nazis
Nazis
  atrocities by, 8, 12, 83–84
  beginning of, 55
  censorship by, 12, 86, 101–102, 103–12, 117, 131
  ceremonies for, 96, 100–101
  children of, 72–84, 87
  Communists and, 14, 20, 23, 24, 41, 85, 89, 105–109
  on crime and criminals, 14, 20, 23–31, 101
  eugenics theories of, 11–12
  euthanasia policies of, 12, 20, 73
  fascination with, 8–9
  industrial practices of, 13–14
  length of regime of, 8, 20
  medical experimentation by, 8, 11–12
  military buildup and, 135–41
  on racial inferiority, 14–15, 56
  police of, 23–31

political opponents and, 14, 20, 24
popular support for, in Germany, 15, 23, 56, 86, 90
prisons and, 14, 20
sterilization programs of, 12, 20
suicide and, 75, 80–81
totalitarian control of, 11–18
treatment of disabled people by, 12, 20, 48
use of capital punishment by, 24–25
use of technology by, 12, 100, 113
see also Gestapo; Kripo; SS
newspapers, 10, 12, 81, 112
Nielsen, Carl, 124–26
Niemöller, Martin, 15–16
Nuremberg Laws, 28, 43, 48–53, 56, 90, 92
Nuremberg Party Congress, 28, 96–97

Olympia (film), 100
Olympic Games, 89, 91, 100, 113, 118, 138

Panassié, Hugues, 132, 134
People's Court, 104
Pick, Gerd Peter, 130–31, 133
Poland
  concentration camps in, 14, 63–71
  Nazis invade, 13, 103, 104, 107, 108, 140
propaganda
  apparatus of, 103–12
  film, 41, 100–101, 104–12
  Nazi, 12–13, 40–42, 50, 59
  purpose of, 100–102, 103, 139, 141

racial discrimination, 14–15, 40, 43–47, 56, 90–91

radios
  German developments in, 9–10
  Nazi use of, 12–13, 85–86, 100, 104, 107, 113
Reichleitner, Franz, 70–71
Reinhardt, Django, 131, 132
Reuth, Ralf Georg, 117
Riefenstahl, Leni, 17, 100
Rise and Fall of the Third Reich, The (Shirer), 96
Rivesaltes camp, 119–20, 129
Röhm, Ernst, 27–28

Salzburger Nachrichten (newspaper), 81
Schirach, Baldur von, 41, 97
Schulz-Köhn, Dietrich, 130–34
Schwarz, Rudolf, 122, 124–26
Sereny, Gitta, 63, 72
Shaw, Artie, 131
Shirer, William L., 96, 107
Sobibor, 63–65, 69–71
Social Democrats, 85, 88, 94
Spanish civil war, 139
speeches
  on economy, 135, 139
  Hitler's, 12, 109–10, 113–18, 135
Speer, Albert, 17, 57, 100–101
SS (security police), 34–38, 73, 74, 80, 123
Stalin, Joseph, 105
Stangl, Franz, 63–71
Stangl, Theresa, 63–71
Storm Troopers (SA), 27–28
Strasser, Hermann, 8
Sudetenland annexation, 138

Third Reich, 23, 24
Treaty of Versailles, 86, 116
Treblinka, 66, 70, 71
Triumph of the Will (film), 100

Übermensch, 9

U-boats, 103, 104
United States, 10, 13, 137

volkisch (Fascist) theory, 29–31
Volkswagen project, 10, 13, 135–36, 139–41

Weimar Republic, 22–23, 89, 92
Weisker, Gertrude, 17
women, Hitler and, 58–62, 106
World War I
effect of, on Europe, 55, 124
effect of, on German economy, 10, 55, 86
World War II
beginnings of, 13, 103
deaths in, 14
Hitler Youth in, 85

youth organizations. *See Hitlerjugend*